15/701 / SFe

Purchased in Santo Fe, NM.
at the Museum of American Indian Art

RE-RIDING HISTORY
Horseback over the Santa Fe Trail

Rancho Arriba, Curtiss Frank's bed and breakfast inn and ranch, lies at the edge of the Kit Carson National Forest, four miles from the Pecos Wilderness boundary and one-half mile east of the village of Truchas, New Mexico. At 8400 feet elevation, it affords a spectacular view of the Sangre de Cristo mountains to the east and the Jemez range to the west. The pointed volcano that can be seen from the porch is the Pedernal mesa painted so often by Georgia O'Keefe. Inquiries are welcome: Rancho Arriba Bed and Breakfast, P. O. Box 338, Truchas, NM 87578. Telephone: (505) 689-2374. E-mail: rancho@roadrunner.com.

RE-RIDING HISTORY
Horseback over the Santa Fe Trail

Curtiss Frank

SUNSTONE PRESS
SANTA FE

Any uncredited photographs were taken by either the author or Jack Underhill.

© 1997 by Curtiss Frank. All rights reserved.
Printed and bound in the United States of America. No part of this book may be reproduced in any form or by any electronic or mechanical means including information storage and retrieval systems, without permission in writing from the publisher, except by a reviewer who may quote brief passages in a review.

Sunstone books may be purchased for educational, business, or sales promotional use. For information please write: Special Markets Department, Sunstone Press, P.O. Box 2321, Santa Fe, New Mexico 87504-2321.

FIRST EDITION

10 9 8 7 6 5 4 3 2 1

Library of Congress Cataloging in Publication Data:
Frank, Curtiss, 1957-
    Re-riding history: horseback over the Santa Fe Trail / Curtiss Frank.
    —1st ed.
       p. cm.
    ISBN: 0-86534-254-7 (pbk.)
    1. Santa Fe Trail—Description and travel. 2. Packhorse camping—Santa Fe Trail. 3. Santa Fe Trail—Pictorial works. 4. Santa Fe Trail—History. 5. Frank, Curtiss, 1957- —Journeys—Santa Fe Trail. I. Title.
F786.F77   1997
987—dc21   96-45607
                                       CIP

Published by   SUNSTONE PRESS
                        Post Office Box 2321
                        Santa Fe, NM 87504-2321 / USA
                        (505) 988-4418 / *orders only* (800) 243-5644
                        FAX (505) 988-1025

CONTENTS

MAP / 6

FOREWORD by Marc Simmons / 7

PREFACE / 9

Chapter 1—Only an Idea / 11

Chapter 2—Outfitting / 29

Chapter 3—Kansas / 50

Chapter 4—A Never-Ending Thirst / 65

Chapter 5—The High Lonesome / 87

Chapter 6—Living in Two Worlds / 130

Chapter 7—The Path to the Present / 197

Chapter 8—Rio Pecos / 217

POSTSCRIPT / 248

FOOTNOTES / 251

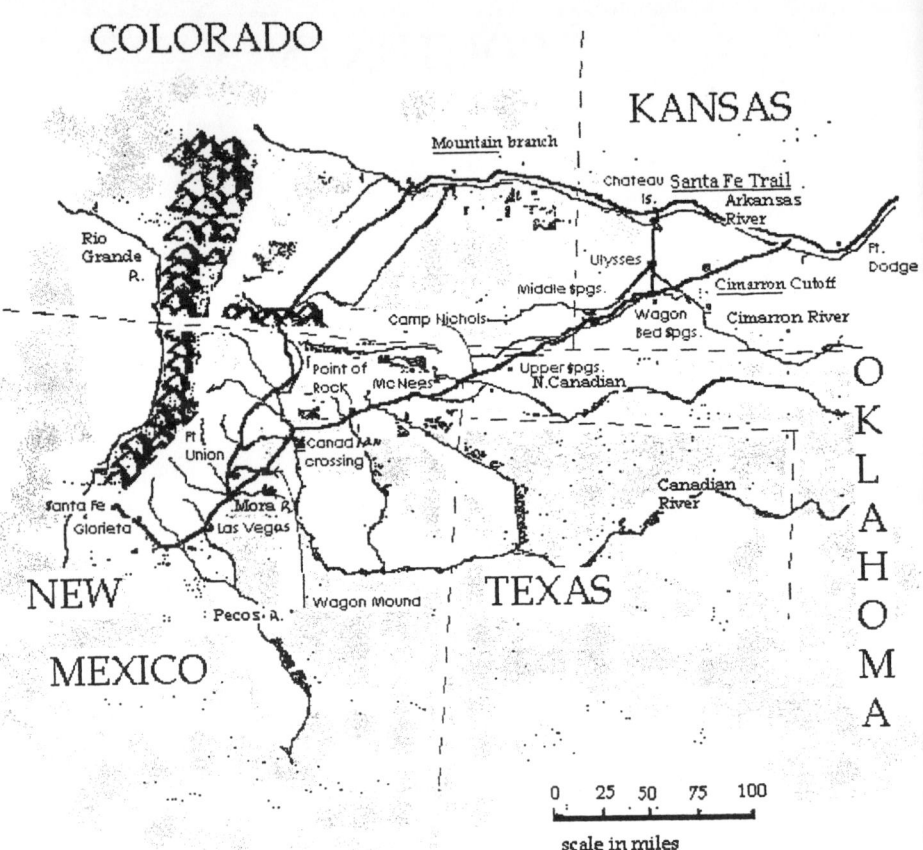

FOREWORD

In the early 1970s, Curtiss Frank and Jack Underhill, a pair of mismatched thirty-somethings who had been chums since boyhood, decided to ride horseback over the old Santa Fe Trail, or at least over a several-hundred-mile section of the far end of it. From the birth of the idea to its actual execution was a long distance, and the result was a throwback kind of adventure that forms the subject of this book.

And the motive for the trip? Curtiss Frank says that reading the many firsthand accounts of the earliest trail travelers stirred up his blood and got him to wondering what it would be like to retrace the original pioneer route, with the aim of reliving the experience and also discovering what physical evidence of the past remained visible. It was a challenging prospect, one that appealed to Jack Underhill, who signed on to form the second half of the expedition.

As the author notes, other adventurers had recently undertaken the same journey, going by foot, horseback, or even wagon. But uniformly, they had elected to use public roads, which today in many places are at a considerable distance from the Santa Fe Trail. What Frank and Underhill proposed was to find the actual historical ruts and stay in them across private ranchland and open country, so as to make a faithful retracing of the authentic route followed by the nineteenth-century freight caravans.

At the time this journey was made, 1972, Gregory Franzwa's useful volume, *Maps of the Santa Fe Trail*, had not yet been published. So Curtiss Frank, who worked out the itinerary in advance, was forced to rely on the rather unsatisfactory trail guides that then existed. But as it happened, once the enterprise was launched, near the town of Ulysses in the southwestern corner of Kansas, events and the routing unfolded in defiance of design and pre-planning.

This story recounts the pleasures, hardships, adventures, and discomforts encountered by two modern-day overlanders who guide their horses over the Cimarron Cutoff of the Santa Fe Trail on an excursion that began as something of a historical reenactment and becomes along the way a life-transforming experience. The reader should note that some of the dangers, physical miseries, and livestock problems confronting our intrepid pair were virtually identical to those dealt with by wagonmasters and teamsters a century before. It is this that adds an extra element of drama to the narrative of Curtiss Frank. Together with personal experience, he weaves in extensive quotes from original trail diaries and chronicles to remind us what the early-day journeys across the plains were all about.

In 1978 I met Jack Underhill on the Santa Fe plaza and first heard the details of the trip now described in the pages of this book. I thought it a fascinating tale then, and reading Curtiss Frank's firsthand account long afterward I find that my initial judgment is confirmed. *Re-Riding History* is a cracking good yarn, and I am pleased to recommend it to all those with a genuine interest in the historic Santa Fe Trail.

—Marc Simmons

PREFACE

This is a book about an adventure. For me it was a life altering experience because I acquired a perspective which led to major decisions about my future and significantly changed my life. I wrote the book in the winter of 1972-73 while living more or less snow bound in a cabin lit by kerosene. I got my water by melting snow once the stream froze. That experience too was a thrill being likewise a routine of simplicity and an economy of the basics.

After that the manuscript was lost, being rediscovered in January, 1995. I have reproduced it on a computer—not a simple or terribly satisfying experience, but rather one of frustration and setbacks to rival the trip over the Santa Fe Trail. However, this was accomplished with the illusion and expense of technological power. Apparently I still haven't learned the lesson.

"I see young men, my townsmen, whose misfortune it is to have inherited farms, houses, barns, cattle, and farming tools; for these are more easily acquired than got rid of."
—Henry David Thoreau: *Walden*

Tienes que cantar como si no te importa el dinero
Querer como si nunca estuvieras lastimado
Bailar como si nadie te mira
Te tiene que surgir el ánimo se quieres salir bien.

—palabras de una canción del campo

—Curtiss Frank
Truchas, New Mexico
1996

1 ∞ Only An Idea

"In 1872 the Atchison, Topeka, and Santa Fe Railroad entered the valley of the Upper Arkansas. In that year, twenty-four years ago, on a delicious October afternoon, I stood on the absolutely level plateau at the mouth of Pawnee Fork where that historic creek debouches into the great river. The remembrance of that view will never pass from my memory, for it showed a curious temporary blending of two distinct civilizations. One, the new, marking the course of empire in its restless march westward; the other, that of the aboriginal, which like a dissolving view, was soon to fade away and be forgotten.

"The box-elders and cottonwoods thinly covering the creek-bottom were gradually donning their autumn dress of russet, and the mirage had already commenced its fantastic play with the landscape. On the sides and crests of the sparsely grassed sand hills south of the Arkansas a few buffaloes were grazing in company with hundreds of Texas cattle, while in the broad valley beneath, small flocks of graceful antelope were lying down, quietly ruminating their midday meal.

"In the distance, far eastwardly, a train of cars could be seen approaching; as far as the eye could reach, on either side of the track, virgin sod had been turned to the sun; the 'empire of the plough' was established, and the march of immigration in its hunger for the horizon had begun.

"Half a mile away from the bridge spanning the Fork, under the grateful shade of the largest trees, about twenty skin lodges were irregularly grouped; on the brown sod of the sun-cured grass a herd of a hundred ponies were lazily feeding, while a troop of dusky little children were chasing the yellow butterflies from the dried and withered sunflower stalks which once so conspicuously marked the well worn highway to the mountains. These Indians, the remnant of a tribe powerful in the years of savage sovereignty, were on their way, in charge of their agent, to their new homes, on the reservation just allotted to them by the government, a hundred miles south of the Arkansas.

"Their primitive lodges contrasted strangely with the peaceful little sod-houses, dugouts and white cottages of the incoming settlers on the public lands, with the villages struggling into existence, and above all with the rapidly moving cars; unmistakable evidences that the new civilization was soon to sweep the red man before it like chaff before the wind.

"Farther to the west, a caravan of white covered wagons loaded with supplies for some remote military post, the last that would ever travel the Old Trail, was slowly crawling toward the setting sun. I watched it until only a cloud of dust marked its place low down on the horizon, and it was soon lost sight of in the purple mist that was rapidly overspreading the far-reaching prairie. It was the beginning of the end...."[1]

The man who wrote these words in 1896, Colonel Henry Inman, had spent his entire career on the Western Frontier. Writing in retirement, he dramatically portrayed the passing period of the Old West which he knew and vividly remembered: the period which saw the isolated French-Canadian trappers and mountain men, rugged men who walked from the Colorado Rockies to California and were at times reduced to such misery that they were forced to eat their beaver pelts, their moccasins, even their horses.* This was a period when the Bents and St. Vrain built their adobe forts and established a trading empire from the Wyoming border to the Mora Valley of New Mexico; the period which saw Indian wars, at first only acts of counting *coup* and the intertribal economics of the plains: horse stealing; but which ultimately, as whites came to occupy the land and exterminate the buffalo, became wars of survival and racism. It was the time of the Santa Fe Trail.

Attracting traders as early as 1812, the trail began to serve regular pack trains in 1821. That year also, Mexico gained independence

---

* *[Sabin in* Kit Carson Days *quotes George Ruxton on the mountain man diet."Meat's meat' is a common saying in the mountains...." and Sabin goes on to describe the consumption of crickets, prairie dogs, buzzards, mules, crows, mountain lions, coyotes, and raw intestines— "wound spirally upon a stick...(and) sucked in like spaghetti." When a group of starving trappers shot an old mustang out of necessity, they lamented the meat "would remain in the stomach for a long time, in a state of indigestion, and for several days (eight or ten, they said), 'they belched up the old stud as strong as ever'"p.153]*

from Spain which led to more favorable attitudes toward *gringo* adventurers. In January 1822 William Becknell rode into Franklin, Missouri with three companions, returning from New Mexico with the profits of their trade. Onto the street they poured the contents of their rawhide sacks: $15,000.00 in silver *pesos*. That expedition was reputed to have yielded a profit of fifteen hundred percent on a small amount of Missouri trade goods. Inspired by profit, Becknell returned to Santa Fe with three wagons and in a dozen years, after an especially wet season, wagon ruts would be indelibly stamped into the plains, becoming a permanent feature of the southwest. In places, the ruts eroded into gullies 15 feet deep, other times appearing as only four slight furrows thirty feet wide running side by side as the wagons drove two or at times four abreast. They remind us that the travelers had to be prepared at the first sign of Indians to pull into a defensive corral.

Wagon train in the 1930's *(T. Harmon Parkhurt, Denver Public Library)*

Riding up over a hill today, one hundred years later, one can still see the ruts stretching endlessly towards the horizon and New Mexico, or gracefully sweeping around the slope of a hill where the travelers endeavored to spare their oxen the more tedious direct ascent. Over the trail rode the innumerable traders, some stopping to camp and immortalize themselves by etching a rock outcropping ("R. Beatty Sept. 20 1865

Dayton Ohio"). The invading American Army marched over that road to occupy the southwest and California in 1846. Union and Confederate troops marched to battle in Apache Canyon and the immigrants traveled this route on their way to the California diggings in 1849. Some were immortalized because they failed to make it ("Isaac Allen 1858"). Until 1880, when the Santa Fe Railroad reached the capital, stilling the rolling wagon wheels forever, the trail was a route of epic importance.

A pioneer wagon *(T. Harmon Parkhurst, Denver Public Library)*

For some reason, although it was primarily a commercial road, and to a lesser degree a military route and path for settlers, the Trail has always seemed the most romantic of the old wagon routes. Perhaps this is due to the combination of Indian adventures and the lure of foreign customs which New Mexico represents. For while Indian attacks threatened all wagon roads in the West, the Santa Fe Trail encroached on the territory of the Kiowas and the Comanches, two of the most fierce and implacable opponents to white voyagers. Although traders and trappers established excellent relationships with other tribes, often marrying into them and rising to positions of leadership in their councils, these particular Indians were regarded as more difficult and unpredictable in their attitudes toward whites.

In the early days, the main route of the Trail's western half, the waterless Cimarron Cutoff passed through their range. Tales of Indian atrocities and attacks commonly surrounded the trail. Indeed, when mountain man and scout, 32 year old Jedediah Smith, was killed at Lower Spring on the Cimarron, it was an event of national significance. Grown rich in the Rocky Mountain fur trade; explorer of the Great Basin, the Mojave, the Rockies and the Columbia, and first white man to cross the Sierras into California; Smith wanted to try his luck in the Santa Fe trade before settling down to write his memoirs. In May, 1831, Smith's party became lost. As Smith himself rode ahead to seek water, he came across a buffalo trail leading to the spring. There the Comanches surprised and shot him. It was reported that he was beaten to death with his own arms. His death provided further evidence for those petitioning for military protection from Indians along the trail. Such protection, granted sporadically at first, soon led to the establishment of the U.S. Cavalry.

On the subject of Indian atrocities, Colonel Inman states:

". . . although having but little compassion for the Indians, [I] must admit that during more than a third of a century passed on the plains and in the mountains, [I have] never known of a war with the hostile tribes that was not caused by broken faith on the part of the United States or its agents."[2]

We must attribute some of the interest in the Trail to the romantic appeal of Santa Fe itself. *La Villa Real de Santa Fe* was the capital and population center of Mexico's northernmost province, its territory including present day New Mexico and parts of Arizona, Utah, Colorado, Oklahoma, and Texas. Spatially, administratively, commercially, and militarily isolated from the rest of Mexico, the province was as highly vulnerable to American penetration as it was to the constant attack of surrounding Indians. Its 40,000 people were primarily engaged in agriculture and were poor. A few rich families controlled government and industry consisting primarily of sheep raising and mining. Since most manufactured goods had to be imported, they were virtually absent. Houses were without window glass, metal hinges, or sawn lumber. Even today in some mountain villages one may see the old wooden latticed window in a house dating from the mid 1700s. Obviously almost anything manufactured would have a market without competition in New Mexico. Cloth, cutlery, mirrors, pans and other hardware, even salt and sugar were shipped there. In return came furs, Spanish dollars, and the animal subsequently associated with the state of its destination, the mule. And half the fun was getting there.

Early travelers described the arrival of their caravan as a source of local pleasure; the population, especially women, turned out *en masse* when the wagons were sighted and "The evening [was] dedicated to dancing and festivity."[3] In fact the region was so isolated that Missouri traders soon found it profitable to extend their trade route as far south as Old Mexico. By 1840 one half of the Trail's traffic went on to Ciudad Chihuahua, and at the time of the American conquest, James Magoffin, the trader who was instrumental in getting the New Mexican army to surrender the Territory without fighting, operated a store in that city. Of *La Villa Real* itself, descriptions and reactions offered at the time seem most related to the moral position of the early traveler. An American observer of Santa Fe in 1831 wrote:

> "To dignify such a collection of mud hovels with the name of 'City' would be a keen irony; not greater, however than the name with which its *Padres* have baptized it. To call a place with its moral character, a very Sodom in iniquity, 'Holy Faith,' (Santa Fe) is scarcely a venal sin; it deserves Purgatory at least. Its health is the best in the country, which is the first, second, and third recommendation of New Mexico by its greatest admirers. It is a small town of about two thousand inhabitants, crowded up against the mountains, at the end of a little valley through which runs a mountain stream of the same name, tributary of the Rio Grande. It has a public square in the centre, a Palace, and an Alameda, as all Spanish Roman Catholic towns have. It is true its Plaza, or Public Square, is unfenced and uncared for, without trees or grass. The Palace is nothing more than the biggest mud-house in the town, and the churches, too, are unsightly piles of the same material, and the Alameda is on top of a sand hill. Yet they have in Santa Fe all the parts and parcels of a regal city and a Bishopric. The Bishop has a palace also; the only two-storied shingle-roofed house in the place. There is one public house set apart for eating, drinking and gambling; for be it known that gambling is here authorized by law. Hence it is as respectable to keep a gambling house as it is to sell rum in New Jersey; it is a lawful business and being lawful, and consequently respectable and a man's right, why should not men gamble? And gamble they do. The Generals and the

Colonels and the Mayors and the Captains gamble. The judges and the lawyers and the doctors and the priests gamble; and there are gentlemen gamblers by profession! You will see squads of poor peons daily, men, women, and boys, sitting on the ground around a deck of cards in the Public Square, gambling for the smallest stakes.

"The stores of the town generally front on the Public Square. Of those there are a dozen, more or less, of respectable size, and most of them are kept by others than Mexicans. The business of the place is considerable, many of the merchants here being wholesale dealers for the vast territory tributary. It is supposed that about $750,000 worth of goods will be brought to this place this year, and there may be $250,000 worth imported directly from the United States. . . .

"Yet, although dirty and unkempt, and swarming with hungry dogs, it has the charm of foreign flavor, and like San Antonio retains some portion of the grace which long lingered about it, if indeed it ever forsakes the spot where Spain held rule for centuries, and the soft syllables of the Spanish language are yet heard."[4]

Such a view of the province was not unusual; indeed the author citing this description calls it "not incorrect." In the end less indignant attitudes prevailed so that the Americans were willing to conquer the city they so detested.

But not all visitors were so uncharitable. Matt Field, arriving at Santa Fe from Taos in 1840 describes it thus:

"There within half a mile of the base of the mountain, a small spot of the vast green plain that spread away before us was dotted with low one-story buildings, reminding us irresistibly of an assemblage of mole hills. As we approached the city and the houses began to shape themselves more distinctly to the eye, the church in the centre, soaring above the surrounding dwellings, attracted our attention. It was built as high and quite as large as any of our ordinary sized meeting houses, and upon examination our surprise was not a little excited to find that these mud walls could possess such strength and durability. It would be perfectly practicable for the inhabitants to build their houses two or more stories high as far as strong walls are necessary for that purpose, and the reason why they are not so built is not, as one would at first imagine, because mud walls are inefficient but because ground is cheap, and the people prefer half a dozen rooms in a row to as many apartments piled one above another. They think it is easier to go through a door way than up a pair of stairs, which is certainly not a very unreasonable conclusion to arrive at. Besides, although time is plenty, carpenters are scarce, and a boarded floor is a luxury for which they entertain not the slightest ambition.

"The apartments are of various lengths but never exceeding twenty feet in width, (the church is an exception) and across walls from side to side are stretched, sometimes good hewn timber, sometimes rude branches, according to the means of the builder. Over these is laid a thick covering of grass and straw, and upon this earth is piled from one to two feet deep, which forms the roof. A very pleasing effect is produced by the grass growing on the tops of the houses, and as all the dwellings are connected it is not uncommon to see children chasing each other the whole length of a street along the house tops. . . .

"A large square, comprising about three hundred square yards is situated in the centre of the town of Santa Fe. The row of houses on one side is occupied entirely by the public offices, the custom house, and armory, and quarters for the military. The other three sides are used for shops for the sale of merchandise brought from the United States, and are kept by Americans. The houses are built of clay, and with very few exceptions are but one story high. Shops are rented to traders in this square, the best situation in the place at from ten to twenty dollars a month. The store keepers, in dull times, sit at their doors all day smoking cigars, cracking jokes with the Spaniards, and peeping under the veils of the *Señoras* and *Señoritas* as they pass. The ladies invariably wear either a veil or shawl thrown over their heads. They wear no hat or other covering for the head, but are never seen, in doors or in the street, without their shawl or scarf. They are all dark complexioned, some of them pretty, but many of them plain, and most of them ugly. Generally, they are but slightly removed from the Indians, and these paint their faces like the Indians, with vermilion, by way of ornament."[5]

Subsequently Susan Magoffin (James' sister in-law), arriving with the invading army in 1846, describes the impact and location of the city, situated in a valley wholly visible from the top of the long hill from which she entered the city (just east of "Santa Fe Trail" or former "College Avenue"):

". . . This leads into the street which as in any other city has squares (being about three blocks by two blocks on both sides of the river) but I must say they are singularly occupied. On one square may be a dwelling-house, a church or something of the kind, and immediately opposite to it occupying the whole square is a cornfield, fine ornament to a city that. A river runs through the place, affording me a fair opportunity to enjoy that luxury to the fullest extent. The church is situated at the Western end, and though I cannot answer for the grandeur of the inner side—to say nothing of the 'outer walls'—I can vouch for its being well supplied with bells, which are chiming, it seems to me, 'all the time' both night and day.... *Nuestra casa* is situated under the shadow of '*la iglesia*' and quite a nice little place it is. We have four rooms including *la cochina*, our own chamber, storage room, and reception room, parlour, dining-room, and in short room of all work. This is a long room with dirt floor (as they all have), plank ceiling, and nicely white-washed sides. Around one half to the height of six feet is tacked what may be called a screen for it protects ones back from the white wash, if he should chance to lean against it; it is made of calico, bound at each edge, and looks quite fixy; the seats, which are mostly cushioned benches, are placed against it— the floor too at the same end of the room is covered with a kind of Mexican carpeting; made of wool and coloured black and white only. In short we may consider this great hall as two rooms, for one half of it is carpeted and furnished for the parlour, while the other half has naked floor, the dining table and all things attached to that establishment to occupy it. Our chamber, at one end of the 'big room' is a nice cool little room, with two windows, which we can darken, or make light at pleasure, and I must say it is truly pleasant to follow after the Mexican style, which is after dinner to close the shutters and take a short siesta; it both refreshens the mind and body; one is then prepared, without fatigue, of the morning's labours, to go about the duties of the evening."[6]

Susan possessed the curiosity and enthusiasm to observe, and had a personal openness toward the native people, that enabled her to overcome the initial shock at some of the physical privations and local customs—a shock shared by other observers. She was therefore able to appreciate the special qualities and virtues of the people she met to an uncommon degree. Thus Santa Fe, if somewhat surprising as a provincial capital, was no more rude than any frontier American settlement, and boasted a good deal more excitement.

Blackfoot Indian camp *(The American Heritage Book of Indians, p. 341)*

Necklace of fingers *(The American Heritage Book of Indians p. 367)*

College Street (Santa Fe Trail) entering town, 1910.
(The Museum of New Mexico)

San Francisco Street, 1865 *(Denver Public Library)*

East San Francisco Street, Santa Fe, 1870's *(Denver Public Library)*

Santa Fe plaza with corn growing *(Denver Public Library)*

East plaza 1870 *(Denver Public Library)*

Plaza corner (Woolworth site) 1870 *(Museum of New Mexico)*

La Fonda (Exchange) hotel, 1909 *(Museum of New Mexico)*

Governor's Palace, Santa Fe *(Denver Public Library)*

Governor's Palace, Santa Fe *(Denver Public Library)*

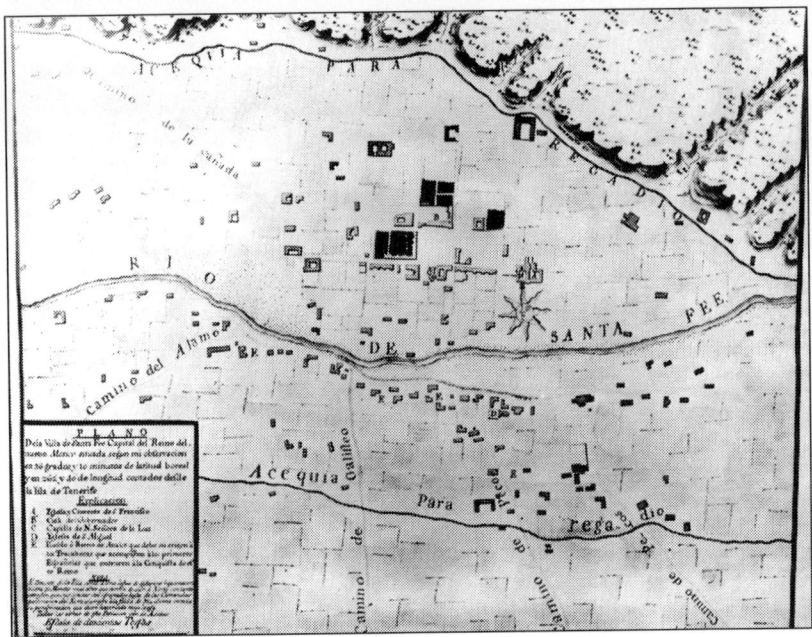

Urrutia map of Santa Fe, 1767 *(Museum of New Mexico)*

Many and varied are the observations of travelers of that period. Some such observations consist of diaries made by travelers on a single journey over the Trail while others are biographies offering more intimate reports of life in those times. A recent massive bibliography on the Santa Fe Trail, compiled by Jack Rittenhouse and celebrating the one hundred and fiftieth anniversary of its opening, lists 350 books, 250 scholarly articles, and more than 100 congressional documents on the topic. Of these more than 700 writings, almost half were by people who traveled the Trail. Many of these accounts are so vivid and exciting that they make the reader want to see the spot where Captain Booth and Lieutenant Hallowell made their frantic escape from the Indians at Walnut creek that morning in 1864; or the place near Point of Rocks where the White party was taken by the Jicarilla Apaches and pursued by Kit Carson and the Army down the canyon of the Canadian, or the battle ground where Confederate troops, on their way to the Colorado gold fields, were decisively turned back outside of Santa Fe. I talked to one old-timer who reported finding musket balls in trees on his property and remembered a battle field cannon on the hill outside of Glorieta where he used to picnic back in 1918.

Having read many striking accounts of the Trail in early days, I began to ponder what it would be like to recreate the experiences of those days in the present times: to take horses or a wagon and retrace the physical experience of the last century. What would it be like today, after so many years? What kind of experience was it to ride on horseback over such seemingly vast distances? What signs of the old *voyageurs'* passing remain? Is it even possible to imagine what it was like that long ago when we are today preoccupied with space travel, vanishing countryside, fast transportation and communication and the constant reminders of our overwhelming human presence: pollution? Many people have followed the roads parallel to the Trail, sometimes only a few miles away, but the feeling of being on the Trail itself must be different. I'd read several of the old accounts, and I began to discuss with a friend from Santa Fe the possibility of traveling the Trail.

Years before we used to take his jeep and drive south out of Santa Fe looking for the old ruts headed for Las Vegas. We once found an old Spanish dam, then silted up, and Indian ruins, like melted loaves of dirt scattered with colorful pottery shards identifying the presence of ancient households or kivas (places housing activities of ancient secret societies). We even uncovered a burial in an ancient garbage heap. The body was drawn up into the flexed position, indicating that burial rites had been performed and that he had been provided with food and utensils in preparation for afterlife. As teenagers, we had had some difficulty sleeping that night camped as we were in the midst of a village abandoned some five hundred years, near a skeleton all too forcefully reminding us of ghosts, which we were too old to acknowledge. All this in a locale where the only reminders of life were the howling of skulking coyotes.

But now, more than twenty years later we wanted to recreate a feeling of history by actually riding the trail. The more we discussed it, the more the ride became an idea to which we could really commit ourselves, and we became excited by the prospects and the challenges. Many questions came to mind. Was the Trail possible to find? And if we could find it, was it possible to follow? Would we constantly run into fences? Would ranchers and farmers throw the interloping trespassers off their land, or worse, take a shotgun to us? How would we supply ourselves and our animals with food and water through unknown territory?

These problems seemed overwhelming as we actually began to make plans; they were so new to me that to prevent some worrisome nights, at times I just refused to think about what we were getting ourselves into. The thought of finding ourselves someplace in Kansas, giving up our vehicles, and having nothing to get us to New Mexico but horses; of (hopefully) following a track in the ground that has been abandoned for ninety-two years through parts of Kansas, Oklahoma, Colorado, and New Mexico, brought about a special kind of feeling ("insanity" hinted some rather darkly) of aloneness and being lost, and yet at the same time gave us an invigorating sense of being dependent on our own resourcefulness, upon the bounty of the land around us, and on the generosity of the people we might meet.

It was a unique feeling for me, one best left unexplored until we were dealing with more tangible circumstances. "And so," as the man used to say, "Return with us to those thrilling days of yesteryear."

2 ∞ Outfitting

Our trip started out being conceived as an historical journey to compare the present with the past. Having read Susan Magoffin's vivid account of an initially romantic encounter with the wild west and foreign southwest which ultimately became a personal encounter with death fears and salvation, and having also studied the writings of Emory[7] and the more matter of fact descriptions of Sibley,[8] we thought it would be exciting to journey ourselves over the road which occupies such an important position in the literature of that part of the country we loved.

Such a ride would be a great personal challenge due to our somewhat decrepit physical states and the mere fact that neither of us had ever spent much time on horseback or were especially good riders. Indeed, while I was beginning to condition myself to riding in the spring, Big Red my horse, had tried to buck me off again and reinjured my chronic back condition, so that I decided to have a complete physical checkup. The result was an order by the doctor to get a brace and give up riding as a form of exercise which he described as the worst possible torture to which I could subject my gentle vertebrae. Being less than enthusiastic at the prospect of losing first the use of my legs, then back, arms, lips and ultimately my eyebrows—all at the age of thirty five—I followed the advice of a friend who knows more about these things than I do and forsook doctors for a chiropractor who promised to have me supple and athletic in a matter of weeks. (He did.) But certainly riding hundreds of miles cross country trying to follow wagon ruts cut into the ground 140 years ago and finally abandoned almost 100 years ago presented logistical, diplomatic and other obstacles.

Basically what we wanted to do was to compare the scenes described by travelers in the last century to what we saw. This meant that we had to find out, first of all, if the Trail was identifiable enough to enable us to follow it cross country, and secondly, if it was physically practical to ride through the locations crossed by the Trail. Initially I decided that the Cimarron (pronounced "Cimarrone" by the natives) route would be the most feasible and in some ways the most interesting route to take. It was the major route in the earliest days of the Trail. Many of the old eyewitness accounts deal with this section of the Trail, the more dangerous due to Indians and the lack of water, but the more direct and easier since it obviates the arduous climb over Raton Pass on the mountain route. Also this route traces the least populated and most unchanged sections of the Trail. In talking to people along the route, I found that the country had been unfenced until the last thirty or forty years, making it practically the same as when the Spanish under Coronado explored it four hundred and thirty one years ago.

Red and friend

Trying to locate the actual path of the Trail without making a life career out of it could prove to be something of a problem. Many general maps show the approximate Trail and Kenyon Riddle's book, *Maps and Records of the Old Santa Fe Trail*[9], contains invaluable mile by mile depictions including scale measurements from certain landmarks. But even these maps lacked sufficient geographical contours to pinpoint the Trail's exact location in many places. It is most useful when trying to locate the Trail from an intersecting road, but unfortunately, there are not many intersecting roads in that country.

I thus decided a reconnoiter was in order, and taking my four-year-old daughter, Eliza, I set out from Santa Fe by car to scout the country. As we drove east toward Clayton on that spring day through the rolling yellow ocher grass lands, occasionally crossing the sweep of indelible Trail ruts sometimes four abreast and gently sculpted into the sod, or passing a great buffalo wallow like an empty plains lagoon describing a perfect circle in the earth's surface, I felt my enthusiasm quicken and my excitement rise at the thought of becoming one with this vast and historic land. I felt then, intuitively, that we would make the trip, that obstacles could be overcome and we would find it possible, indeed compelling. Subsequent conversations with people along the route, in which they conveyed their enthusiasm and interest, were to confirm the early stirring which the Trail aroused in my languishing spirit of adventure. It was a very powerful experience.

We knew that the Trail followed or ran parallel to either the Santa Fe Railroad, or in a general way Highways 85 and 56 through New Mexico, Oklahoma, and Kansas, and indeed the towns along U.S. 56 have had it designated the "Santa Fe Trail Memorial Highway" and have formed the "Santa Fe Trail Highway Association" to promote tourism. This local agitation had included an occasional modern caravan of wagons and riders traveling over the highway. But we were interested in a more exact route in order to get the most accurate "feel" of the Trail, and in most places the highway is ten miles away from the old Trail itself. This means that in the southeastern corner of Colorado, for example, there is no road parallel to the Trail within thirty miles. But I reasoned that if we were unable to follow the Trail itself, as a second best alternative we could follow the highway or road way right-of-way. (This turned out to be chimerical thinking as we were later to find out.) I thus set out to find as detailed county maps as possible in hopes that these country roads might more closely follow the Trail's route. In some places there were a few dirt roads although their stair step pattern would add greatly to the distance traveled.

In trying to locate more detailed maps I was sometimes able to get large county maps and compare them to Riddle or ask local people approximately where the Trail crossed various people's land. The Agriculture Department has some maps based upon aerial photographs which show the Trail and which are available to ranchers. (Unfortunately early efforts to secure one of these in Boise City, Oklahoma, failed and it wasn't until we were actually on the Trail later that I found out from a rancher exactly how to go about obtaining them.) After looking at county maps and talking to local people in Clayton, New Mexico and in Oklahoma, across whose land the Trail passed, I concluded that it would be possible to identify the Trail by its remains frequently enough to make it practical, using the maps we had, to just strike out cross-country and watch for ruts.

There remained the problem of permission to cross private land. In looking at the county maps and plotting land ownership at the county clerk's office, it was obvious that such a ride would involve crossing land belonging to many hundreds of different people. After talking to some land owners and hearing of one local newspaper editor's experience making such contacts with land owners in one county, it was decided to simply cross the land and take our chances, just being sure not to leave gates open or to decorate the landscape with our Trail Chef food packages. When we encountered a land owner we would just tell him what we were doing and rely on his anticipated mercy. Thus I finished this sojourn with some vague plan of operation, convinced that at least from a geographical standpoint the trip was feasible, and was fired with enthusiasm to relive a bit of history.

As the Santa Fe railroad reached Dodge City, Kansas, in Fall 1872, eliminating the eastern end of the Trail (the Kansas Pacific Railroad, about 70 miles north, had already reached Colorado and cut heavily into civilian Trail traffic) we decided to begin around Dodge, thereby retracing that part of the Trail that was still in operation one hundred years ago. This would take us across the dreaded *Jornada* or Waterscrape, approximately fifty miles of "Cimarron desert" which stretched between the Arkansas river (the U.S.-Mexican boundary) and the Cimarron, and had cost the life of Jedediah Smith. This was a somewhat disturbing prospect because we did not anticipate being able to carry much water—certainly not enough to supply horses laboring through summer heat. Inman, describing Becknell's first efforts to pioneer this route, relates his experience on the Jornada:

> "His temerity in abandoning the known for the unknown was severely punished, and his brave men suffered untold misery, hardly escaping with their lives from the terrible straits to which they were reduced. Not having the remotest conception of the region through which their new trail was to lead them, and naturally supposing that water would be found in streams or springs, when they left the Arkansas they neglected to supply themselves with more than enough of the precious fluid to last a couple of days. At the end of that time they learned, too late, that they were in the midst of a desert, with all the tortures of thirst threatening them.
>
> "Without a tree or a path to guide them, they took an irregular course by observations of the North Star, and the unreliable needle of an azimuth pocket-compass. There was a total absence of water and when what they had brought with them in the canteens from the river was exhausted, thirst began its horrible office. In a short time both men and animals were in a mental condition bordering on distraction. To alleviate their acute torment, the dogs of the train were killed and their blood, hot and sickening, eagerly swallowed. Then the ears of the mules were cut off for the same purpose, but such a substitute for water only added to their sufferings. They would have perished had not a superannuated buffalo bull that had just come from the Cimarron River, where he had gone to quench his thirst, suddenly appeared, to be immediately killed and the contents of his stomach swallowed with avidity. It is recorded that one of those who partook of that nauseous fluid said afterward, nothing had ever passed his lips which gave him such exquisite delight as his first draught of that filthy beverage."[10]

And Josiah Gregg, Tennessee born, graduated from medical school, and yet while still in his twenties so chronically sick he was barely able to leave his room for a year, when he was sent across the prairie to regain his health, described the perils of the Jornada less than a decade later:

> "Our route had already led us up the course of the Arkansas River for over a hundred miles, yet the earlier caravans often passed from fifty to a hundred farther up before crossing the river; therefore nothing like a regular ford had ever been established. Nor was there a road, not even a trail, anywhere across the famous plain extending between the Arkansas and Cimarron rivers, a distance of over fifty miles, which now lay

before us—the scene of such frequent sufferings in former times for want of water. It having been determined upon, however, to strike across this dreaded desert the following morning, the whole party was busy in preparing for the water scrape, as these droughty drives are very appropriately called by prairie travelers. This tract of country may truly be styled the grand prairie ocean: for not a single landmark is to be seen for more than forty miles—scarcely a visible eminence by which to direct one's course. All is as level as the sea, and the compass was our surest, as well as principal guide.

"For the first five miles we had a heavy pull among the sandy hillocks; but soon the broad and level plain opened before us. We had hardly left the river's side, however, when we experienced a delay of some hours in consequence of an accident which came very near proving fatal to a French doctor of our company. Fearful lest his stout, top-heavy dearborn should upset whilst skirting the slope of a hill, he placed himself below in order to sustain it with his hands. But in spite of all his exertions the carriage tumbled over, crushing and mashing him most frightfully. He was taken out senseless and but little hopes were at first entertained of his recovery. Having revived, however, soon after, we were enabled to resume our march; and in the course of time the wounded patient entirely recovered.

"We now moved on slowly and leisurely, for all anxiety on the subject of water had been happily set at rest by frequent falls of rain. But imagine our consternation and dismay when, upon descending into the valley of the Cimarron on the morning of the 19th of June, a band of Indian warriors on horseback suddenly appeared before us from behind the ravines—an imposing array of death-dealing savages! There was no merriment in this! It was a genuine alarm—a tangible reality! These warriors, however as we soon discovered, were only the van-guard of a countless host, who were by this time pouring over the opposite ridge, and galloping directly towards us.

"The wagons were soon irregularly formed upon the hill-side: but in accordance with the habitual carelessness of caravan traders a great portion of the men were unprepared for the emergency. Scores of guns were empty, and as many more had been wetted by the recent showers, and would not go off. Here was one calling for balls—another for powder—a third for flints. Exclamations such as 'I've broke my ramrod'—'I've split my caps'—'I've rammed down a ball without powder'—'My gun is choked; give me yours'—'were heard from different quarters; while a timorous greenhorn would perhaps cry out, 'Here, take my gun, you can out-shoot me!' The more daring bolted off to encounter the enemy at once, while the timid and cautious took a stand with presented rifle behind the wagons. The Indians who were in advance made a bold attempt to press upon us, which came near costing them dearly; for some of our fiery backwoodsmen more than once had their rusty but unerring rifles directed upon the intruders, some of whom would inevitably have fallen before their deadly aim had not a few of the more prudent traders interposed. The savages made demonstrations no less hostile, rushing with ready sprung bows upon a portion of our men who had gone in search of water; and mischief would, perhaps, have ensued had not the impetuosity of the warriors been checked by the wise men of the nation.

"The Indians were collecting around us, however, in such great numbers that it was deemed expedient to force them away so as to resume our march, or at least to take a more advantageous position. Our company was therefore mustered and drawn up in line of battle and accompanied by the sound of a drum and fife we marched towards the main group of the Indians. The latter seemed far more delighted than frightened with this strange parade and music, a spectacle they had no doubt never witnessed before, and perhaps looked upon the whole movement rather as a complimentary salute than a hostile array; for there was no interpreter through whom any communication could be conveyed to them. But, whatever may have been their impressions, one thing is certain - that the principal chief (who was dressed in a long red coat of strouding, or coarse cloth) appeared to have full confidence in the virtues of his calumet; which he lighted, and came boldly forward to meet our warlike corps, serenely smoking the pipe of peace. Our captain, now taking a whiff with the savage chief, directed him by signs to cause his warriors to retire. This most of them did, to rejoin the long train of squaws and papooses with the baggage, who followed in the rear and were just then seen emerging from beyond the hills. Having slowly descended to the banks of the stream, they pitched their wigwams or lodges; over five hundred of which soon bespeckled the ample valley before us and at once gave to its recently meager surface the aspect of an immense Indian village. The entire number of the Indians, when collected together, could not have been less than from two to three thousand — although some of our company insisted that there were at least four thousand souls. In such a case they must have mustered nearly a thousand warriors, while we were but little over two hundred strong. Still, our superior arms and the protection afforded an equality in point of valor. However, the appearance of the squaws and children soon convinced us that for the present at least they had no hostile intentions; so we also descended into the valley and formed our camp a few hundred yards below them. The *capitanes*, or head men of the whites and Indians, shortly after met and, again smoking the calumet, agreed to be friends.

"Although we were on the very banks of the Cimarron, even the most experienced traders of our party, whether through fright or ignorance, seemed utterly unconscious of the fact. Having made our descent far below the usual point of approach, and there being not a drop of water found in the sandy bed of the river, it was mistaken for Sand Creek and we accordingly proceeded without noticing it. Therefore, after our big talk was concluded and dinner dispatched we set out southward in search of the Cimarron.

"We continued our march southward in search of the lost river. After a few miles' travel we encountered a ledge of sand hills which obstructed our course and forced us to turn westward and follow their border for the rest of the day. Finding but little water that night and none at all the next day, we began by noon to be sadly frightened; for nothing is more alarming to the prairie traveler than a water-scrape. The impression soon became general that we were lost—lost on that inhospitable desert, which had been the theater of so many former scenes of suffering' and our course impeded by sand hills! A council of the veteran travelers was called to take our emergency into consideration. It was at once resolved to strike in a north westerly direction in search of the dry ravine we had left behind us, which was now supposed to have been the Cimarron."[11]

Shortly before this, in 1829, the U.S. Government had provided the first military protection of the traders on the Trail. After increasing Indian attacks upon the trains (some say in response to an incident following the killing of McNees and Monroe), President Andrew Jackson authorized military escorts of the Santa Fe trade. It provided escort as far as Chouteau's Island on the Arkansas River, (in the western part of present day Kansas) and as the *Jornada* represented the Mexican frontier, the American infantry was thereupon restricted to marching back and forth camping along the Arkansas awaiting the caravan's return in October. Except for an initial excursion into the Mexican Jornada the soldiers spent a frustrating two months watching mounted Indians raid and steal their cattle and (officers') horses, for they were unable to do battle except with cannons from a distance. (Their next escort, four years later, would be by Mounted Rangers, which that same year became the U.S. Cavalry.)[12]

Soldiers and traders keeping diaries of the events during that historic summer describe their experience in the Jornada. Otis Young offers an account of that same caravan commanded by Charles Bent as it departed the protection of Major Riley's military escort:

"Thereafter, the caravan of 1829 had gone its way rejoicing until it began to travel through the deep sand hills on the west bank of the Arkansas. After nine miles the sand so impeded the wagons, stalling many teams, that the train was extended over a length of more than half a mile. Although no danger was anticipated so close to the escort battalion, Bent had heeded Riley's advice to the extent of sending out sixteen men to ride to the crests of the sand hills on either side of the depression through which the train traveled so slowly.

"At that moment three men of the advance point halted and dismounted to drink. Instantly, Indians by the hundreds began to pour over the crests of the sand hills, quirting their ponies down the slopes and out of the deep ravines. The advance guard hastily scrambled for their mounts, to begin a dash back to the head of the train, only some three hundred yards away. The two who were mounted on horses managed to get away, but the third, Samuel C. Lamme, who rode a mule, was quickly overtaken and filled with arrows. As he tumbled into the sand, the Kiowas stripped him and cut off his head while the rest of the train looked on helplessly.

"As the rush of the shrieking Indians seemed about to submerge the train, Charles Bent rode out alone to check the attack, managing to divert the Kiowas from their headlong dash into the confused traders. Meanwhile his brother, William, had succeeded in outracing another party, but without slacking his pace came immediately to Charles Bent's assistance as Waldo and Jacob Coates, an old hunter, looked on. Back in the wagon train, some of the traders were struggling frantically to cut the crippling lashings about a small cannon and bring it into action. This was finally done in time to aid the hard-pressed Bents. When the match was applied to the touchhole, the Indians took fright, having an unconquerable aversion to wagons shooting at them, and 'they would raise their heads above the hills and dodge back like a timid man dodging a streak of lightning' at the discharge.

"Meanwhile, the tired battalion of soldiers was enjoying a well-earned rest on the banks of the Arkansas. Cooke wrote in the 'Journal' that the buffalo had vanished, probably due to the rains filling up the prairie water holes, rendering visits to the river unnecessary. As a result, the camp was short of meat, but a day or two of clear weather undoubtedly would remedy that matter.

"Cooke, himself, was enjoying a quiet rest on that hot afternoon, until he '. . . saw beyond the river a number of horsemen riding furiously toward our camp. We all flocked out of the tents to see, and hear the news for they were soon recognized as traders. They stated that the caravan had been attacked . . . that some of their companions had been killed, and they had run, of course, for help.' Riley, in the 'Report', said that the message arrived about 6:30 p.m., stating, '. . . that Mr. Lamme, a merchant of Liberty, was killed, and they were only six miles off, and the Indians were all around them, and if I did not go to their assistance they expected to be all killed and scalped.'

"Riley had little time to hesitate. The only really serious consideration which might have militated against his aiding the traders was the fact that the scene of the attack lay within Mexican territory, and he could not predict how the proverbially thin-skinned Latins would react. If they protested the intrusion, and it was very likely that they might, Riley's career would be ruined. Apparently, Major Bennet Riley considered this incidental when weighed against the frantic demands of the traders. He gave the order to march."[13]

The troops reached the caravan and the Indians withdrew, but for the next forty days the traders continued to be harassed, so that they:

". . . seldom obtained more than three or four hours sleep out of twenty-four; men became worn down with toil by day and watching by night that they would go to sleep and fall from their mules as they rode along. For forty or fifty days we were not permitted to take off our clothes or boots at night, and all slept with their pistols belted around them and their guns in their arms. In several instances men seized their knives in their sleep and struck them into the ground, and the men became afraid to sleep together, for fear of killing each other in their sleep."[14]

Later, bolstered by the addition of a party of 120 Mexicans, they learned that 2000 Indians were waiting for them in a *cañon* (apparently the Canadian) ahead. A party of forty trappers tried to break through from the Taos side to assist them, but was driven back. Returning to Taos the trappers recruited fifty-five more, and after another battle with the Indians managed to reach the caravan, which then proceeded on to Santa Fe.

Upon returning to its rendezvous with Riley on the Arkansas, the caravan was accompanied by a Mexican military escort under Colonel José Antonio Viscarra. The party of twenty-nine wagons, two pieces of artillery, and almost 300 men and women encountered no problems until they reached the Cimarron (probably at Willow Bar). There, according to a Mr. Bryant, of the party:

"About sunset, just as we were preparing to camp for the night, the sentinels saw a body of a hundred Indians approaching; they fired at them and ran to camp. Knowing they had been discovered, the Indians came on and made friendly overtures; but the Pueblos [Indians] who were with the command of Colonel Viscarra wanted to fight them at once, saying the fellows meant mischief. We declined to camp with them unless they would agree to give up their arms; they pretended they were willing to do so, when one of them put his gun at the breast of our interpreter and pulled the trigger. In an instant a bloody scene ensued: several of Viscarra's men were killed, together with a number of mules. Finally the Indians were whipped and tried to get away, but we chased them some distance and killed thirty-five. Our friendly Pueblos were delighted, and proceeded to scalp the savages, hanging the bloody trophies on the points of their spears. That night they indulged in a wardance which lasted until next morning."[15]

According to Young who offers another account of the same event:

"The traders not only scalped alive one Indian, but skinned several, and Cooke saw one of these skins still stretched on a wagon side. The barbarity of the whites disgusted even the hardened Mexican regulars. Ten scalps in all were recorded as having been taken; the Mexican escort lost a captain and two privates in the encounter."[16]

A great deal of history is associated with the Jornada. But today it is hard to imagine an ever present possibility of hostile Indians along the route. Yet I can sympathize with what must have seemed at times an overpowering danger. As a kid, me and a bunch of other guys endured an "Indian raid" in the mountains. Huddled in our open cabins at night, for the savages obligingly disappeared during the day to regroup and commit their depredations elsewhere, we were told that the area was cut off from the outside world, nearby villages had been destroyed, and that it looked like a fight to the death. This sort of encouragement went on for several nights, each night the attackers getting closer and more open in their presence. (I learned to sleep on my stomach figuring that it was easier to take being stabbed in the back than in the soft flesh of the belly.) One of the adults in our camp had a pistol which he fired with a great roar from behind the shutters occasionally shouting that he had hit one of the demons. In would fly an arrow which we'd gather around and examine, quivering at the sight of its stone point.

The older members of our encampment served as leaders, but boys in several cabins organized into squads and selected their own chiefs. Somehow, during one of those organizational meetings, I got chief of my group, probably because I appeared most scared and so in the best position to represent all of us. I think my duties included scouting the hillsides around the camp—a duty which never even seriously crossed my mind to perform! I especially recall the last night as one of brazen terror. At dark, we cowered in our cots, the usual drumming and carrying on began in the woods. But this time, high up on the mountain some half-mile across the lake upon which our open-sided cabins were situated, a series of bonfires began to glow. Watching this ominous portent, we were next startled by a volley of burning arrows, fired from the mountainside down towards the lake (and us, although we were out of range). Not really taking comfort in their distance from us we soon realized the purpose of this action, when suddenly a series of torches lit up on the shore opposite us revealing war canoes filled with Indians. We watched helplessly as they slowly moved across the water towards our camp, a man in the bow and a man in the stern of each canoe holding a burning torch which cast eerie light and sent an ominous message across the waters.

About the time they hit the bank a little way down shore, I had decided I'd had enough and orders or no orders, chief or no chief, I was getting out. I groped from my bed toward the open side of the cabin porch into a scene of utter confusion. People were running back and forth shouting. I think guns were going off and I remember clearly Indians mixed with the crowd, sometimes darting into one of the cabins. Somebody grabbed me and asked me what I was doing there, but I can't recall whether or not I was articulate at that point. I think he told me to go back to bed which even at the time occurred to me to be the advice of an imbecile and raised permanent doubts about all forms of authority. My response was to crawl under the cabin where I spent about as much time as I could spend alone in this time of burning, looting, and killing.

I thereupon removed myself to the next cabin where I was first greeted with terror, and then, when it was learned that I was one of the children and not a fiendish savage come to add havoc to the already demoralized situation, I was welcomed like General MacArthur returning to the Philippines. One of the demons had come through their cabin and dumped over a bed the occupant of which was now safely cached in bed with another, to the intense relief of both. The question was for whom was I to provide the next salvation? (They were all under the mistaken impression that I was very brave to be the only one wandering about, an impression I don't recall correcting, for their utterances began to make me feel at least as brave as they had been for remaining in bed.) In this way I passed the last night of siege, which then mysteriously ended without any of us figuring out why. If, on the Jornada, we had to deal with the problem of water, at least we did not have to deal with Indians.

If the threat of hostile natives, thirst or trackless desert provided contrast between the *voyageurs* and ourselves, our present state of disorganization and fumbling was a definite point in common. From looking at maps and talking with people along the route it seemed that the extensive presence of windmills meant that we would be able to find enough water along the route and that we wouldn't have to carry more water than what our canteens held. So in addition to our camping equipment, we had to organize our food supply, keeping it light enough to carry, obtain necessary horses and buy a pack saddle. As there were very few towns along the way, we would have to carry everything we needed with us. For this reason, as well as economy, it seemed reasonable to plan and purchase most of what we would need ahead of time. For, as we were to find, even if a town was visible across the prairie some ten or fifteen miles away, this kind of an aside was still a full day's ride for us!

The planning process proved to be our first great stumbling block and threatened to break up our ship of venture before we even started. For my partner is, as his mother has put it, a "child of God," and when it comes to possessions, planning, or organizing, exhibits a carefree spontaneity and indifference which is occasionally charming but in these circumstances was totally exasperating. Akin we are in spirit, but in practical detail we are as unlike as the worlds of poesy and power. And while we have these things to learn from each other on occasions of luxury and abundance, during our preparations for this survival test he forced me into the unwelcomed role of Prussian drillmaster.

Added to this ironic juxtaposition of conflicting natures in which the contrasts were highlighted to a point of appearing to be character disorders, was the fact that Jack was completing a book some months behind his anticipated schedule and was preoccupied with the mechanics of final draft and publication. Having gotten off work in early June, I came down from Colorado to my cabin in New Mexico where Jack had been living for the past nine months writing his book. Most of his time went into writing or driving to Albuquerque to visit his typist for proofreading.

So as the summer weeks ticked away, we were still unprepared with horses, food, or finances. I had procured the pack saddle, and through the sudden windfall of another friend's aborted boat trip down the San Juan river, acquired a month's provisions of dried food, all arranged and packaged into daily rations for two (although judging from the packages it appeared they ate like six.) This was a bonus badly needed at a time when our efforts were sagging. Another week's frustrating search in the local villages for suitable horses capable of handling the arduous trip turned up a pair reputed to be both strong and *mancito* (broken) at the place next to mine. Trying out the horses, Jack chose the one whose gait and temperament he favored. But when he wanted me to go and do the negotiating for him, that was the last straw. As I was already lending him the money to make the trip, I left him enough to get the horse and repaired up into the mountains for a few days of sylvan retreat with a *novia*, prepared to leave on the trip by myself if he didn't. When I returned we had acquired "Old Jeanie" and at last we were poised for our departure eastward to Kansas.

Our camping gear included our packs loaded with two changes of clothes, including boots and warm coat, a poncho, candle lamp and flashlight, mess kit, writing materials, camera, sleeping bag and mattress. Our baggage contained an axe, two rifles and pistol, cook grill, farmer's leather kit, a water bag and two canteens, shovel, tarpaulins, binoculars, those books about the Trail which we considered most important to have with us, two tents, portable radio, recorder and guitar, booze, a stove, oil for saddles, thirty foot leads, hobbles, and other equestrian necessities. Through experience we were to learn just what we required and just what we could live without! In addition we carried thirty days' worth of dry food for us and grain for the horses. We anticipated needing to supplement the meager grass supply with grain because of the heat and amount of work the horses would be doing.

In the old days the stock was frequently so worn out they had to be abandoned at the end of the trip because of the limited nourishment they received in relation to the size of their efforts, and we did not want any such result. For anyone anticipating a similar trip, a little information on our experience with food might be useful. Specialty dried foods are quite expensive and for the most part, barely edible. Many of the items, such as milk, are available at chain groceries much cheaper and they are frequently better tasting. Based upon our experience, I would recommend a combination of the few decent specialty dried items, such as stroganoff and sandwich mixes, together with more commonly available items from the grocery which may not be as conveniently packaged, but are more satisfactory. For a typical menu I suggest:

Breakfast: powdered eggs, bacon bar, fruit drink, milk, Ovaltine, Tang, coffee, sugar, or for a lighter meal, cold cereal concentrates, dried fruits.

Lunch: sandwich mixes are quite good, e.g., Trail Chef, and melba toast or solid bread loaves that won't crunch, flour tortillas, dried fruits, sour juices, jello (to be drunk) and jerky, candy bars (that won't melt) like tropical chocolate, and fruit bars—look at supplies of a health food store.

Dinner: bouillon powder (watch out that the dried soups are not just potato starch, flavor and color—they're vile), stroganoff, stew, beans (here some canned goods can be pure luxury) dried vegies, instant puddings (if you can stand flavored cornstarch).

Many times little additions such as olive oil in eggs or bacon bits in baked beans, can make these items seem delicious. We used bouillon powder in lots of things, hot chili sauce for meat, lemon juice in fruit drinks. Even a short supply of fresh fruits or vegetables makes a lot of difference, and something liked chopped carrot or celery makes a good substitute for lettuce in sandwiches. Bread should be carried in some sort of rigid container and if not, should never be presliced. We found the most fantastic drink in the early days of the trip (while it lasted) to be Start (orange drink) and grain alcohol. It lacks the impurities of vodka, is cheaper, has a pure taste, and elevates the spirit without poisonous baddies the next day.

These are foods we settled into using after some pretty startling disappointments, and food, like rest, provided our principal resource under very stressful conditions. It was very important to both our level of energy and our feelings of psychological well being; more important, I was to discover, than I had ever realized in my superabundant, overserved, civilized life.

Because my truck could only carry two horses (Big Red and Jeanie), and since we wanted to avoid further horse shopping and having to get a trailer to haul our pack horse, we decided to take our chances and buy a pack horse when we got to Kansas, a prospect I did not relish as it had taken us a delay of three weeks to get things done which we had been anticipating for months. Too, my horse had thrown a shoe the day after being shod in Colorado and Jeanie needed shoeing so we would have to do that as well. There was no point trying to do it locally because the previous year I had spent two months trying to find a local blacksmith, and had only crippled up my back when I finally found someone and had to help him hold the kicking, lunging Red. There was no way I was going to risk that scene again. Jack was going to have to get a poncho and bridle and we were in need of a few other sundries, so I dreaded further lost time.

On Sunday, July 2, we made our final preparations to leave the next day. We gathered all our baggage and divided it into what we would need right away and what we wouldn't. We decided to take two vehicles and leave one near Clayton, New Mexico, approximately half way between our departure point and destination. It would contain part of the supplies so that we didn't have to carry everything, and if we got into some emergency along the way, we would have a vehicle to support any course of action decided upon. (Like quitting!)

Typical of our disagreements was the "great umbrella tent caper." In May Jack came up to Colorado to do some planning on the trip. In shopping for supplies he had discovered an umbrella tent on sale which was tall enough to stand up in, could sleep five, had netting, floor, and all the other accouterments of a Holiday Inn. Jack decided that this tent, which was reminiscent of Knights Templar and Ivanhoe, lacking only the parading tourney, regal streamers, and political intrigue, was perfect for the trip.

"Oh sure," I said, "and it will only use up 175 lbs. of our 150 lb. weight, and one pannier which it's too big to fit into."

"Nonsense," he said, "it only weights 60 lbs., and the salesman guarantees that it will fit into (he should have said 'fill up') the size of our pannier."

I said "No way in hell are we going to haul something as superfluous as a tent that size four hundred miles over the Santa Fe Trail by horse back. And besides, I already have an umbrella tent that is just what you want because it is the same size, only bulkier and heavier, so it would be even more impractical." I was planning to sleep outside anyway not in a goddam canvas womb and if it rained I had a two-man army tent that would do just fine. But he said he had always wanted a tent like that and when it rained we would want some place where we could stand up and move around and I'd see, we'd be glad we had it along.

Remembering his penchant for impromptu buying, I stood firm. (We were halving our purchases with joint ownership.) I remembered when we were kids how he did his shopping out of the Johnson-Smith novelty catalog, just as other people are loyal to J.C. Penney's. In those days he came up with a slang dictionary which, when we opened to find the dirty words, began "Atta boy," Atta girl," "that's the boy," "that's the girl."

And when he sent off for the prison pennants ("decorate your room now," "Sing Sing," "Alcatraz") and he hung them from the molding around his room, they were six inches long! He was the only person I've known to actually send in his $2.98 to Station XERF, Del Rio Texas, for this amazing double-your-money-back guarantee-offer of 99 hit recordings, all by the original artists. And when they came they were on the organ and he didn't get his money back. I didn't want to own half of *that*. So we compromised. He'd buy the tent for himself and take it along and we'd see if we used it. So he hit me up for the sixty bucks and that's what we did.

That Sunday we spent packing and repacking the umbrella tent. I would put it way in the back of the saddle niche, with the other things in front where we could get to them when we needed them. He would unpack the things and repack them in the back, putting the tent in front where we could get at it when we camped. I would put the tent poles back under the saddles and canned goods, tarp and neatsfoot oil, and he would unpack them and put them on the front seat where we could grab them as soon as we got there. And so it went.

Meanwhile the horses were passing their last uneventful day grazing. We had put them in a neighbor's pasture where the grass was better for the last few days feeding. It was more food than Jeanie had seen all winter, but she was not impressed. Jeanie was a big-boned black with a face that came from the cartoons—fleshed tucked in all the way around her jaw and snout, beginning behind the nostrils, similar to the head of a pig. She had thrown a colt in the spring and that combined with the absence of grass had left her boney and angular, with the appearance of Rosinante. Estimates of her age had ranged from 12 to 16, but she was reputed to be strong and had a long, sure stride. Unfortunately, her colt had not been weaned by this time and even now was grazing along the road with the rest of Audelio's ponies. Sometime during the morning they had wandered by the pasture; and when we went to check on her, there was a big hole in the fence. After searching the area up to the forest, we found them idling along the road. We returned Jeanie to the pasture but fenced out of sight of the road, to the whinnying cries of the whole bunch.

Monday morning we were up at dawn to load for an early start. I was somewhat apprehensive about getting the horses into the van because the last time I had tried to load Red, bringing him from Colorado to New Mexico, his resistance had taken two and a half hours to overcome. That time I had to ride him up the ramp and into the van. At first I had tried it bareback, and he had "commenced to buckin'" as the old timers put it, and so I had to saddle him up to get him in. And there was the time I had loaded him with another horse and was getting ready to climb out of the van when they started jumping around. I leaped to the front by their heads just as the other horse went down onto the floor. That's when things really started to happen. Both horses were panic stricken, the fallen horse thrashing about, trying to get up, with Red leaping up and down half beside and half on top of him, and me jumping around trying to avoid all those hooves like steel punches from Mohammed Ali. We were like three stones, two big ones and a pebble, all together in a tin can which someone was trying to shake up into a big bloody Margarita! Well, I made it through that one alive and was out of shock less than four hours later (after I got through loading them up again to bring them back home), but I was not looking forward to this new opportunity with Red and a new horse about which I knew nothing. (I won't go into the many other exciting events in which I had participated with Big Red in the year since I had bought him, but they began with such an auspicious encounter that one of the first things I did was to have him castrated. While I won't say it put us on an equal footing, it helped establish a *rapprochement*.)

That day we started with Jeanie, who was a bit diffident about the whole process. As we began to coax and pull, we collected a unique audience: the rest of Audelio's herd. About the time we got her in and tied, her colt, figuring no doubt that his mother had been devoured by an Alpo processing truck and was soon to come out as a dog food patty, gave a whinny of alarm and out came Jeanie, flying low, disguised as a crashing black blur. From then on out it was out of our hands. We tried everything we could think of but a shoe horn.

We blindfolded her, we tied ropes around her butt and tried to pry her in, we tried to drag her, and whip her, and drove the truck to the side of a hill where, if she fell down the slope, she would slide in. We even led Red in, easy as you please, hoping she'd follow, but it wasn't to be. At three in the afternoon we finally said the hell with it, we'll get Audelio to load his goddam horse in the morning after she'd had a night to settle down. By then we couldn't even get the colt away from her and so had to take her and his herd down to his pasture, lead them all in, and then try to cut her out by herself. But it seems that was not to be either. Every time we tried to separate her, the colt would slip in by her. Finally I took my lariat and roped the colt, tying him to a fencepost. As we took her out he made a dash for her and broke the post off at the ground, ripping it loose from the barbed wire fence. Then he started racing around in circles, stirring up a cloud of dust created by the leaping, bouncing fence post and scattering the other horses as he swept by. There was no way I was going to catch him and get my rope back, and I'm sure he'd be there yet racing up and down but for the fact that as he sailed around the pasture puffing with increasingly labored breath, the noose was slowly tightening around his neck. When he finally fell over on the ground, he was hissing and wheezing and his eyes were bulging out of his head making him look like he was ready to expire, which, from my point of view, would have had its satisfactions about then.

Audelio came over the next morning at seven thirty and we started again. Having let the horses loose to graze near the truck by the road, we came down the hill to find Red standing by the fence next to three or four strands of loose barbed wire and no sign of Jeanie. Worse yet, when we followed her trail, it was marked by drops of blood where she had cut herself going through the wire. Another fine day to start!

We found her in the next pasture, looking for her colt, a nice gash cut into her hock. Jack was verging on the disconsolate, but we determined that it was not so deep to be crippling and treated it. Then we prepared to load her. Beginning patiently, Audelio, her former owner, reasoned with the horse.

"Come on, Jeanie, come on, old girl," as he pushed and pulled and he pushed and I pulled, and he pushed and we pulled, and we pushed and they pulled; he began to get angry.

"Come on, goddammit, Jeanie. Come on, Jeanie," and his voice inclined upward ever so slightly, for Audelio is not one to lose his cool.

"Come on, Jeanie, wrap the rope around both bars as I push her in!" I instructed as I drew the rope in, wrapping it around the steel brace of the van. With every inch gained against her four implanted legs, the halter stretched longer, and her head separated further from her body and her eyes seemed to be looking back behind her as she came. So tight were her forequarters that it was as though Audelio was back there wrestling with a different animal in the rear and Jeanie was a spectator, straining, but unable to see from her confined vantage point all the shoving and struggling motions between man and beast going on back there.

"Come on, *Jodido* bastard," and then she went, as though going for the roof and escape, lunging and tossing and tearing, and I release her a few inches. Back went her feet and out the side over the ramp. I was standing on the running board by the driver's side looking over the side into the van while pulling on the lead rope to draw her in. Beside me and below, the driver's door was open. Jack and Audelio were behind her at the rear of the truck. As she came out they scattered and I dropped to the ground ready to run. Jeanie flew out half twisted and trying to get around the side of the truck where I was holding her lead rope. As she passed the

Jack Underhill

edge of the loading ramp, she lost her footing and went over the side, her body crashing to the ground beside the truck and her head taking off the tail light as it passed.

As she came rolling down the hill toward me, I turned to run and crashed straight into the open door. Stunned, I fell back against the truck, and when I looked up from her head Audelio was at her tail. Jeanie was stretched out on her back lounging in her partial freedom, her four legs in the air and milk squirting from her teats in a graceful arch three feet into the air and over onto the side of the truck where it dribbled down into a dangling liquid collage. I looked up as Audelio and I caught each other in a moment of stumbling, angry, frustration spilling into mirth at the incredible sequence of events; but good form kept us from collapsing into hysterical laughter and we struggled to control the convulsive hilarity which threatened to advertise our exposed foibles. I let go of the rope allowing Jeanie to struggle to her feet, and we led her around to the back pretending nothing out of the ordinary had occurred. But now and then a sudden smile or an uncontrolled laugh would burst out as we renewed the struggle in its newly created context of that absurd image. To keep up the pretext, she had to go in fast and Audelio seemed to pick her up and carry her in.

By eight o'clock they were loaded and Jack disappeared to write it up. Out into the rain, over the snowy pass to Mora. We were on our way.

3 ∞ Kansas

It was overcast as our caravan of two vehicles headed north on the Taos road and then turned east at the Rio Pueblo. Clinging to the side of the cliff as we crossed the mountains, we were enveloped in the ground fog. Rattling along, we were unable to see more than a few feet as we passed an occasional sign identifying a scenic overlook. Light snow fell on the highway and the horses shifted uneasily in the back of the truck as we rounded a curve in the road. Suddenly the view cleared. In the road ahead were a dozen cars stopped by a small landslide which had heaped rocks and debris across our lane. I slammed on the brakes, doing my best to avoid throwing the horses up into the manger. As we slowly threaded our way through the clear area, I wondered what would have happened if this had occurred a few yards previously where the fog was still settled upon the road.

Mora. Sapello. Las Vegas. We stopped briefly at the Santa Fe Trail museum in Springer and talked to the interested personnel about our pending trip. Headed east through Taylor Springs, close to where the Trail crosses the Canadian (Red) River at a place called *El Vado de las Piedras*, the day was darkened by a flat, gray sky which occasionally condensed into a torrential rain, afterwards breaking up into a few drizzling clouds extending to the distant horizon.

Much later we stopped for food at Clayton where boys in high brimmed, straw cowboy hats, pleated boots and belled jeans discussed one of the numerous local rodeos currently going on there. Standing in line in his synthetic double knit slacks, Red Wing boots, and Spencer Tracy felt hat, Jack turned to me and said, "Yore not from around these parts are ya, stranger?" A few miles out of the town of Moses where the trail crossed State Highway 18, we found a farm house where we could leave the car.

Nearby was McNee's Crossing, where a historical marker announced the first known celebration of the Fourth of July on the Plains which were to become American. Josiah Gregg described it:

"The second day . . . as we lay encamped at McNee's (Currampaw) Creek, the Fourth of July dawned upon us. Scarcely had gray twilight brushed his dusky brow when our patriotic camp gave lively demonstrations of that joy which plays around the heart of every American on the anniversary of this triumphant day. The roar of our artillery and rifle platoons resounded from every hill while the rumbling of the drum and the shrill whistle of the fife imparted a degree of martial interest to the scene which was well calculated to stir the souls of men. There was no limit to the huzzas and enthusiastic ejaculations of our people; and at every new shout the dales around sent forth a gladsome response. This anniversary is always hailed with heart-felt joy by the wayfarer in the remote desert; for here the strifes and intrigues of party spirit are unknown: nothing intrudes in these wild solitudes to mar that harmony of feeling and almost pius exultation which every true-hearted American experiences on this great day."[17]

Shades of more uncomplicated times. It was 1831, exactly 141 years earlier to the day.

As the afternoon wore on we began to speculate how far we were going to get before dark. It was best to find a place, unload, and set up

---

Santa Fe Trail Museum Notes

John Underhill from Santa Fe and Curtiss Frank from Ft. Collins, Colo. were visitors in the Santa Fe Trail Museum recently. Mr. Underhill and Mr. Fdank were on their way to Dodge City from Truchas, New Mexico (where they have a cabin), to ride the Santa Fe Trail, staying with the Trail as closely as possible. They are hauling two horses for riding and will buy a pack horse in Dodge City. Total personal equipment with packsaddle and grain will weigh about 200 pounds.

Mr. Underhill and Mr. Frank expect to reach Santa Fe by the end of July.

Underhill is a Photo Journalist, most recently managing editor of news at KGGM-TV in Albuquerque and author of "The Search for Maggie", a Western Movie. Frank is a Sociology Professor at Colorado State University.

They will colloborate on a book up-dating chronicles on the Santa Fe Trail or the many photo plates. They are doing it mostly for the pleasure of it, the idea being in the making for a year.

"Springer Tribune" July 13, 1972

camp while it was still light, for there would be no moon tonight. But we knew that if we unloaded Jeanie there was a good chance we would not get her back in the truck again so we resolved to go as far as we could. At Boise City we took a wrong turn and headed north into Colorado. I was sleeping and Jack hadn't traveled the route before, so when I awoke to the unfamiliar country we were forty miles out of our way.

We needed to reach a town which was large enough to find someone to shoe the horses and where we could buy a pack horse as well as other supplies we needed. It was getting dark now as we drove east through what had been the *Jornada*. Occasional flashes of lightning mixed with the bursts of rockets from the fireworks' displays appeared on the horizon.

We decided to head for Ulysses, 75 miles west of Dodge, on the north fork of the Cimarron (Sand Creek to Gregg's party), near the site where Bent's party, accompanied by Major Riley, had battled the Kiowas in 1829. But when we arrived it was too late to rouse anyone who could provide us with a place to unload, water the horses, and camp. After fruitless dealings with the sheriff and other local characters and a drive into

The burning wheat fields

the country looking for a place to camp, we left the horses in the truck and found a motel room, tired and considerably discouraged by the whole series of events. Maybe a bath and a good night's sleep. . . .

The next morning the horses, tired of the whole thing, were up early. Consequently, we were up early and so was everyone else in the vicinity. Clanking around in the back of the truck, they seemed determined to communicate their desire to vacate in spite of our bribes of water and grain. Under the watchful and disapproving eye of the motel manager, we piled into the truck for the ten-mile haul to the river and greener pastures. The rain had caused the usually dry North Fork to flood and muddy water was standing all over the bottom. Reaching the river bridge, we turned onto a dirt road and drove through the tall grass and down to the shallow flowing Cimarron. It was perfect water, grazing, wood and level ground. Our luck had changed and things were looking up. Within a matter of hours, we had located a pack horse, arranged for shoeing and were out collecting supplies.

Now we began to get reaction to our pending trip. We talked to Jerry Sullivan, who operated the grain elevator where we bought concentrated feed for the horses.

"Why," he wished aloud, "I've always wanted to take a trip like that. If I could only drop everything right now and ride along with you boys!"

And Ev Stutzman, who sold us some tack and a Palomino horse, remarked, "He hasn't been used much, so I'd ride him a few days before trying to pack him." His son, Jerry, had to hogtie him to give him his first shoes and loading him out to our camp was Jeanie all over again.

Ev told us the story of his Brahma bull, so big and so gentle that he used to ride him in parades in Ulysses. He provided the kind of fun gimmick that comes along once in a lifetime and is something to be looked forward to. But the rest of the year the bull had to be fed and couldn't be used for anything, so when a friend offered to buy him and pay for his keep, lending him out for any parade for which Ev wanted him, Ev jumped at the chance.

"Why not save the cost of feed, and I can still use him."

But that winter the big bull ate some bad feed and laid down and died. That was the end of Ev's parade riding, and a bit of meaning had passed out of his life, never to be replaced. I could sense his sadness in that experience. I guess a lifetime could be milestoned by a few such small events as this. It was the beginning of what was to prove one of the most rewarding aspects of the trip. Drawing out people we met, seeing some unusual flavor of their lives, some special contact we didn't expect but which seemed to emerge out of the unusual circumstances of our meeting.

For instance, there was the encounter with the clean-shaven rancher who drove his pick-up by our hobbled horses, looked us over with a tinge of suspicion and an unspoken, "Who are these hippie bastards camping on my land?" Later he wound up quartering and tending our horses, giving us bed, bath and food, and we spent the evening squatting around a whisky bottle on the grass by the bunk house, sharing observations about what makes work meaningful and life satisfying.

It always seemed that despite initial diffidence, the knowledge that we were actually riding horseback over the Santa Fe Trail, that we were taking our chances with weather and work and living out of doors close to the land as these people did, provided an identity and established an unusual acceptance. And often when we were struggling with our ineptitude or stumbling in adversity, people responded with generosity, interest, and more of themselves than I was used to. It was as though we had returned to a time when people's similarities were more important than their differences, when appreciation, hospitality, and shelter were expected and granted because there were so few of us.

We saw this appreciation on the roads. Everyone either waved or stopped to talk when they saw us riding down a dirt road with loaded horses. On the small state highways they turned to look or waved so that we looked forward to crossing these few contacts with civilization. It provided acknowledgement which we had not expected, but was a small source of satisfaction. On the larger interstate highways cars sped by with occupants preoccupied and unnoticing, an occasional blank face turning to look. And beside the highway, the train of the Santa Fe passed by in its overdue flight to Albuquerque, "Amtrak" lettered on the sides of cars proclaiming our latest efforts to salvage a piece of pre-isolation travel. Faces from the observation cars peered past us without expression, one, two, three, four, until the last car where a child looked at us with surprise and excitement and began waving. As the train passed into the distance, a lone form hailed us in a single act of human contact.

The two and a half days spent in our first camp on the Cimarron were days of work, accomplishment and optimism. Because of the heavy summer rains that year, the normally dry river flowed lightly, providing water for the horses, and there was plenty of tall grass for grazing. We spent the days lounging in the big umbrella tent, oiling our saddles and equipment, watching the great fires of the burning stubble fields send billowing black cumulus clouds thousands of feet into the sky like a dramatic grandchild of the once common prairie fires, or talking with some of the few visitors who came by the camp to work or watch our preparations. There was an air of relaxed excitement surrounding our anticipated departure. None of the insects or expected rattlesnakes came to disturb our smooth-flowing regimen.

On Thursday, July 6, we got ready to leave. Working out in the sun produced instant sweat so we promised ourselves a last couple of cold beers, loaded the truck with the few things we weren't taking with us and headed for town. Leaving the truck at Stutzman's, we caught a ride with him back out to our camp. As he was connected with the local Ulysses

Shoeing the horses

The tent of contention

radio station, he recorded an interview with us once we reached camp. How did we get the idea for the trip? What were we doing for food? What problems did we anticipate?

"If I had the time, I'd get a few of the boys and stage an Indian raid on you."

Jesus, just what we need! It was a thought that was to return occasionally to haunt me and remind me of just how little we were doing to actually recreate the trip.

At last we were on our own, with nothing but the horses and ourselves to rely on in getting from here to Santa Fe. It was an exhilarating feeling; now that we were actually there it seemed that everything was going to be okay. We packed up Jeanie with our stuff, we weighed the two loaded panniers to make sure they were balanced, strapped the tent across the top, added fifty pounds of grain, wrapping it up in a tarpaulin and hitching it up with rope, the guitar on top of that, then the cooking grill, and water bag. Jeanie buried under a mountain, but it was solid and we took off.

As yet we had not seen the Trail which was angling in from the lower crossing (the Caches) and was to join the river somewhere near our present location. On Highway 270 across the river and south a couple of miles was a sign and historical monument to Jedediah Smith (1798- 1831) saying he was killed near this spot. The sign read:

> "Wagon Bed Springs. Two miles southwest were the Lower Springs of the Cimarron, an 'oasis' in dry weather where shortcuts of the Santa Fe Trail converged to continue up the river. The most popular cut-off turned southwest from the Arkansas River in present Gray County. The 60-mile stretch between the two rivers, known as the 'Jornada,' was a perilous route for men and animals in the dry seasons when wagon trains often ran out of water. Here also fierce Plains Indians frequently attacked and plundered the caravans. Near here in 1831 the noted Western explorer and fur trader, Jedediah Smith, lost four days without water, was killed by Comanches just as he reached the river.
>
> "Late in the history of the Trail a wagon box set in the water gave the springs their name. Little remains of the famous camping place, but wheel tracks of the old Trail may still be seen in near-by areas."

A fence to the north and a steep ravine to the west make it necessary to cross the river and proceed west along the south bank. I was riding Red and leading Jeanie; Jack rode on the Palomino, which I called Linda because he reminded me of a girl I knew, "blonde and unbroke". We crossed the river, which now stank with black effluent from one of the nearby feed lots, and struggled up the south bank into the tall weeds. Wallowing through the underbrush and burrs, which were so thick as to obscure the ground, we followed the river until striking a fall of timber which was too thick to cross. We turned south and proceeded around it until we came to a fence. Giving Jack the lead rope for our pack animal, I rode ahead to find a place to cross, struggling through the sand and crashing into gopher holes until it became obvious that there was no gate and we were going to wind up back at the road headed in the opposite direction.

We decided to recross the river where we had seen a gate and ride through the field above the river which was more clear of brush. We reached the field only to realize that we had lost the tarp back across the river. Jack said to leave it, but if it rained we would need it so I retraced our steps and searched for it. Nothing made me happier than to ride through all that brush and stickers again, but I was lucky enough to find the tarp where we had first crossed the river. Great tying job, I thought, congratulating myself on our mastery of packing. I rejoined Jack and we started trotting to make up our lost time. Then began the sequence of events that was to occupy our efforts for the next week, immobilizing us for almost three more days.

As Jeanie trotted along the pack rolled back and forth across her back like a great distended goiter, then it began to shift. The first thing to go was the guitar, which flopped down beside her, hanging tenuously at her side. Suddenly, Jeanie stopped dead, becoming as mobile as a planted tree. Jack, holding tight to the leadrope, was caught off guard. As Linda moved on, Jack began to serve as anchor rope. Gripping Linda with his knees, he tugged at the pack horse. But instead of moving Jeanie, he began to lift Linda's front quarters off the ground. Up in the air she went, as if rearing in defiance instead of confusion. As I caught the event from the corner of my eye, Jack was poised in the air, hanging horizontal on Jeanie's lead rope, his arm outstretched and his opposite foot the only thing in the saddle. He was suspended like a tautly-stretched hammock, and then, crash, dropped between the horses and onto a convenient cactus, which, being the only one in the vicinity, had obviously been expecting him. Yes, things on this side of the river were definitely superior. To make a long story short, we rode around finding all the gates locked, had to stop and adjust the pack every few minutes, broke the strap on the canteen, lost the water bag and camp grill, and when we struggled into our next camp at dusk, it was getting ready to rain. We had traveled a grand total of one mile!

The next two days were the nadir of our packing accomplishments. We struggled with hondas, lash cinches, diamond and half hitches until we were dreaming about them. Once again we set out to relearn the art of "profanity-expending Mexican *arriero*." We had Joe Back's book, complete with all his homilies, on how to do it all. We had practiced before leaving New Mexico and had even packed the big tent into the mountains with no problems, but now that it really counted, now that people were standing around watching us get ready to leave, now that we wanted to pack fast for an early start before the sun began to fry our brains, our diamond hitches now looked like safety pins, our jerk lines sagged like wet laundry, and our cinches cleared the horses' chests and left room enough for a Volkswagen to pass. Through it all Jeanie rolled her eyes in bathos. To simplify things, Jack specialized in diamond hitches and I specialized in half hitches. Taking the copy of *Horses, Hitches and Rocky Trails*, he would pop it open to the diagram on page 84 ("Tie you own diamond hitch,

Jim Bridger used it!") and start laying loops around the pack. Then we'd begin discovering all sorts of nuances and confusions which hadn't bothered us before. Were we drawing the right rope up through the diamond loop? Should we twist the side loop before pulling it around the pannier? Are the breech and breast collars too loose? And page 85 had a Double Diamond! We tried not to look. Then we'd lead Jeanie down the trail, carefully at first, holding our breath. The real test came when the horses started to trot. The pack would start to shift, slightly at first, something would drop off, or the saddle would roll ominously. Back to page 84.

And hot? The sun was so enervating that there were times of day when we just couldn't work. In the morning when the sun hit the tent, the temperature would go up forty degrees until you had to get up. At least our camp had a large corral, which meant that the horses could be penned at night to keep them around, and three big water tanks for stock. When we weren't drinking out of them, we were bathing in them. It was the only way to get refreshed in the unrelieved prairie heat. In this camp the insects began to be a problem. It was the fireants on the ground and the mosquitoes in the sky. (In Kansas, mosquitoes are not the ordinary type people are used to in the United States. They are from another world. They are carnivorous, consuming flesh with a draught of blood; and they swarm so thick that they carry landing lights and are equipped with radar. And once that sun went down it was "gimme shelter." A bite from one of those hummers raised contours which, if in the right place, would be coveted by a Hollywood producer, the appendage being just about as permanent.) It was not what our first camp had been.

Saturday afternoon we decided to change tactics. Jeanie had a good back for packing, a high backbone and all, but the only success we had had so far was with Red, so why not pack him and ride the other two? Jack could ride his horse, and I could ride the Palomino. It wasn't what I had in mind but okay. That horse was close to being mean: he would bite, buck, and kick, and there was no telling what his gait was like (we found out later; a corrugated country road). So I saddled him up and tried to get on him. I think he was bucking before I hit the saddle; anyway, that did it. All I needed was to destroy my back after the first mile of the trip; that would be more than I could rationalize away. At least Jack weighs fifty pounds more than I do and that s.o.b. would never throw him. (Yesterday didn't count; Jack was off guard.)

So we began again, this time with Big Red. Pack everything up, put everything else away. Out comes page 84, throw the old loops, pull the rope tight, don't give any slack, pull that diamond wide, beautiful. Now I come over and do my famous double half hitches. Old Joe Back would be proud. While we still have a few hours' daylight, we'll move up river a couple of miles to Wagon Bed Springs, and it will give us a chance to be sure of our packing. Saddle up the other horses and we're off.

> Walking along and the saddle looks fine.
> Walking along and we're makin' good time.
> Trottin' along, it's a hundred yards now,
> Trottin' along and it's . . . Oh no! Oh, WOW!

The saddle has toppled to the side and it's sliding under Red's belly. Suddenly he's going crazy, like there's a two hundred pound mountain lion clinging to his stomach and he can't figure out how it got there but he wants out of this arrangement. The rope snaps. He's pulled loose and he's taking off. Got to catch him. Get off our horses, grab the rope, settle him down. You hold the saddle up, while I undo it. We drag it clear and tie him up. We can laugh now, but I can tell you that at the time it looked like the end of our last chance, and we can see the trip receding beyond the distant Kansas horizon. We don't say anything. There's nothing to say. Jack's dejected for the first time and I can see he's given up. Time passes and then I say, "There's two things left we can do." (This, fortunately, was not one of the times I was ready to give up or there would have been three.) "We can strip our pack down to just what we consider essential, and trying loading what's left. If that doesn't work, we'll forget the pack horse, carry just what we can get on our own horses, and travel light and fast. Let's forget the whole thing for now, go to town and get the truck, set up camp and start over tomorrow."

I could see him brighten at the possibility of a more decisive move which might finally resolve our dilemma. I crossed my fingers that one of these two courses, though considerably less comfortable, would get us on the Trail, and that, after all, was what it was all about. Our enthusiasm renewed, we stashed our gear, hitchhiked into town and picked up the truck. Fortunately it was late and no one we knew was around so public humiliation was not added to our day's accomplishments. So again we set up the umbrella tent (I was glad to have it now), spread out all our gear for inventory, cooked dinner, and killed a quart of whiskey. In my stupor

I recalled Inman's description of packing back in the 1800s. Had I remembered it earlier, I might have found some solace. His account allowed for human failure.

Wagon Bed Springs, 1972

"A description of the equipment of a mule train and the method of packing, together with some of the curious facts connected with its movements, may not be uninteresting, particularly as the whole thing, with rare exceptions in the regular army at remote frontier posts, has been relegated to the past, along with the caravan of the prairie and the overland coach. To this generation, barring a few officers who have served against the Indians on the plains and in the mountains, a pack-mule train would be as great a curiosity as a hairy mammoth . . . . A pack-mule was termed a *mula de carga*, and his equipment consisted of several parts, first, the saddle, or *aparejo*, a nearly square pad of leather stuffed with hay which covered the animal's back on both sides equally. The best idea of its shape will be formed by opening a book in the middle and placing it saddle-fashion on the back of a chair. Each half then forms a flap of the contrivance. Before the *aparejo* was adjusted to the mule, a *salea*, or raw sheepskin, made soft by rubbing, was put on the animal's back to prevent chafing, and over it the saddle-cloth, or *xerga*. On top of both was placed the *aparejo*, which was cinched by a wide grassbandage. This band was drawn as tightly as possible, to such an extent that the poor brute grunted and groaned under the apparently painful operation and when fastened he seemed to be cut in two. This always appeared to be the very acme of cruelty to the uninitiated, but it is the secret of successful packing; the firmer the saddle, the more comfortable the mule can travel, with less risk of being chafed and bruised. The *aparejo* is furnished with a huge cruper (rump harness), and this appendage is really the most cruel of all, for it is almost sure to lacerate the tail. Hardly a Mexican mule in the old days of the trade could be found which did not bear the scar of this rude supplement to the immense saddle.

"The load, which is termed a *carga*, was generally three hundred pounds. Two *arrieros*, or packers, place the goods on the mule's back, one, the *cargador*, standing on the near side, his assistant on the other. The *carga* is then hoisted on top of the saddle if it is a single package; or if there are two of equal size and weight, one on each side, coupled by a rope, which balances them on the animal. Another stout rope is then thrown over all, drawn as tightly as possible under the belly, and laced round the packs, securing them firmly in their place. Over the load, to protect it from rain, is thrown a square piece of matting called a *petate*. Sometimes, when a mule is a little refractory, he is blindfolded by a thin piece leather, generally embroidered, termed the *tapojos* and he remains perfectly quiet while the process of packing is going on. When the load is securely fastened in its place, the blinder is removed. The man on the near side, with his knee against the mule for a purchase, as soon as the rope is hauled taut, cries out, '*Adios*,' and his assistant answers '*Vaya*.' Then the first says again, '*Anda!*', upon which the mule trots off to its companions, all of which feed around until the animals of the whole train are packed."

Nowadays we use buck-type pack saddles over which we hang a canvas pannier, one on each side. The panniers are open bags with leather hangstraps, which when packed, hang open at the top to combine with the center of the saddle and form a broad platform, upon which bags or tents, etc., can be placed. A long strap from the outside of one pannier then reaches across the load and buckles to the outside of the other pannier, tying the whole load together. Over this, we throw a pack cover and secure the whole thing with a lash rope tied with diamond hitches. At least we try.

Inman continues:

"An old-time *atajo* or caravan of pack mules generally numbered from fifty to two hundred, and it travelled a *jornado*, or days march of about twelve or fifteen miles. This day's journey was made without any stopping at noon, because if a pack mule is allowed to rest, he generally tries to lie down, and with his heavy load, it is difficult for him to get on his feet again. Sometimes he is badly strained in so doing, perhaps ruined forever. When the train starts out on the Trail, the mules are so tightly bound with the ropes which confine the load that they move with great difficulty; but the saddle soon settles itself and the ropes become loosened so that they have frequently to be tightened. On the march the *arriero* is kept busy nearly all the time; the packs are constantly changing their position, frequently losing their balance and falling off; sometimes saddle, pack, and all swing under the animal's belly, and he must be unloaded and repacked again.

". . . Sometimes in traversing the narrow ledges cut around the sides of a precipitous trail, or crossing a narrow natural bridge spanning the frightful gorges found everywhere in the mountains, a mule will be incontinently thrown off the slippery path, and fall hundreds of feet into the yawning canyon below. Generally, instant death is their portion, though I recall an instance, while on an expedition against the hostile Indians thirty years ago, where a number of mules of our pack-train, loaded with ammunition, tumbled nearly five hundred feet down an almost perpendicular chasm, and yet some of them got to their feet again, and soon rejoined their companions, without having suffered any serious injury."[18]

Saturday's big decision: what to leave. Will we need the ax? The small stove? We decide to eliminate a camera, all but one gun, extra tarp, booze, all but one book on the Trail, some food, boots, etc. We're down to 120 pounds. We run the truck up to the nearby feed lot, load the stuff up front and lock it up. "Check the doors, Jack." We catch a ride back to the horses and we're on our way. This time to stay! It's a little after noon and hot as we thread our way along the pair of dirt ruts running between the tree lined Cimarron bottom and the rolling, grass-tufted hills to the north. We are heading west again, past a lone spreading oak tree and around a fence corner reaching up towards us from the river. The heat, boosted by a slight afternoon breeze, is rolling across the prairie. The river bends and we turn south as, looking up the gradual hill to our right, we see the tracks of the Santa Fe Trail which here reached the climax of its wandering across the *Jornada* and struggled into the relief of the Lower Springs. The tracks are broad and there are several sets of them. They are eroded several feet deep as they come down the side of the hill into a cut-away bank and the shelter of the trees. I lope up the hill to get a better look at the passage of the ruts across the prairie and their descent into the valley of the Cimarron. They're nine feet apart, and are cut some thirty inches deep; weeds and brush grow in them, but there is no mistaking what they are. I ride down again leading the pack horse. Jack is taking pictures. We have found our North Star which is to guide us for the next four hundred miles.

Wagon Bed Springs, 1930's (*Denver Public Library*)

4 ◐ A Never-Ending Thirst

Wagon Bed Springs! Known as Lower Springs, in those days; it was the site of Smith's brutal murder and an oasis for all those who took the "upper cutoff" from Chouteau's Island. Chouteau's Island was named for a St. Louis trader who forted up against the Pawnees there in 1816. It was reputed to be the Pawnee's first experience with American guns. The Island marked the shortest route across the *Jornada*. It was here that Riley had camped when escorting the traders in 1829, and under his protection one of the traders (Bryan) recovered $10,000 in silver which had been cached here the previous year. Surveying the Trail in 1825 for the U.S. Government, George C. Sibley wrote the following entry in his Journal:

"Wednesday, 28th, September

"Morning fair, cool, windy. Started at 30 minutes past seven and steered due South. We traveled over a most beautiful plain, so perfectly smooth that the Wagons were as easily drawn over it as they could be over a Bowling green. The Soil is poor, however, producing tolerable grass only here and there, it is all thickly set, however, with short grass. Passed some more Ponds soon after we left camp, and after we had gone 12 miles came to a small creek [North Fork of Cimarron], the water standing in Pools. Its course when running is to the Eastward and runs into the Semerone. Twelve miles farther, we struck the Semerone just below what is called Lower Spring. We were detained butchering a Buffalo Cow that I shot right on the road, so that the wagons did not get to camp till dark. Here we found the Water and pasturage exceedingly fine. The Creek Water is brackish and makes a sort of Salt Meadow of a great part of the level flat watered by it.

"Thus it turns out that the southern extremity of the Sands where we passed them, it is 26 miles due South to the famous Semerone Spring, over a most excellent road, and that the greatest distance without water is 12 miles. The day was tolerably cool, but rendered very unpleasant by a strong and unceasing South wind.

"Courses and distances today, South 12 miles to 12 M. Creek, and then South 12 M. to Semerone Spring. Latitude of the Spring, 37°-24'00", as well ascertained by observations of Aquilae."[19]

Sibley's detailed observations, like those of his companion, Brown, would have been invaluable guides to subsequent travelers. But despite his descriptions and accurate mapping, the documents were lost in Washington for more than one hundred years.

It was a wet year when Sibley went through and his easy passage across the Waterscrape was not often duplicated. But his observations do illustrate what a remarkable difference climatic variations can make in the Southwest. 1972 was also wet, and although we suffered from heat and thirst, the horses were provided for better than usual due to a regularly flowing stream and ample pasturage. Travelers up to this century describe the Spring as a barren section of the river with a marsh on the north side. But two floods have seeded the area in this century, and today

tall cottonwoods surround the small dry rocklined hole, making it seem truly sylvan shelter. The pack was holding well so we decided to push on up the river and see how far we could get today. As we rode away from the spring the tracks disappeared to be discovered again half a mile ahead. Because either cultivation or the absence of erosion had obscured sections of the Trail, we established the practice of anticipating where the easiest passage for wagons would have been in the old days. This usually meant drawing a straight line from a northernmost bend in the river to the most distant observable bend. In this way we almost always managed to intercept the ruts on some gradual slope which produced the erosion necessary to identify the Trail.

It was a beautiful day with a slight haze that gave a sea-like quality to the broad, flat landscape. As we rode on, the trees marking the river bottom thinned out to an occasional cluster in the sandy bed. We could see the river stretching endlessly ahead with its countless meanders adding to its distance. As we passed a lone, wind-swept house with a hard mud road running to it, a Mexican boy ran out after our horses.

"Where are you going to?"

Our recreation

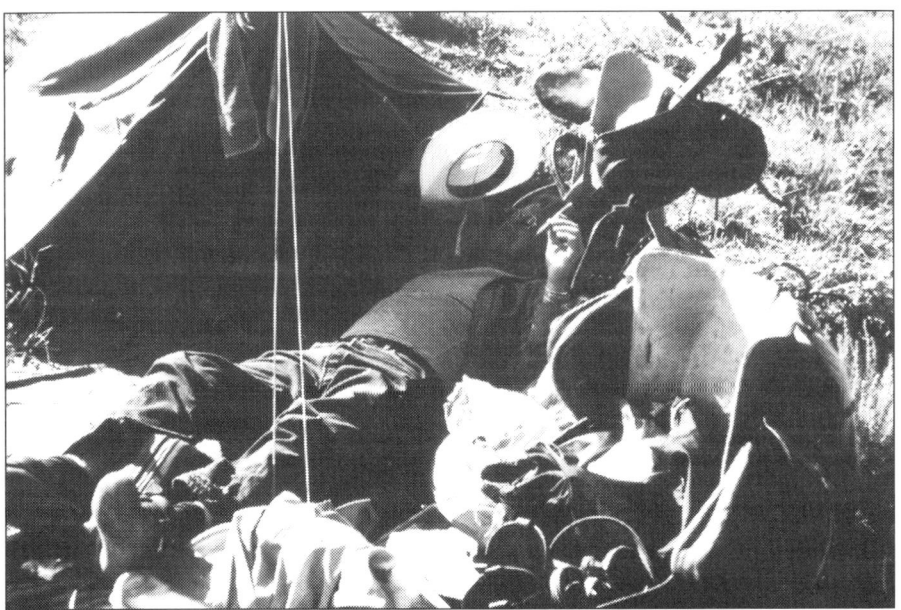

Getting started was difficult

"Santa Fe", came the answer.
"Why are you going there?"
"We're riding the old Trail."

And we left him standing in the road watching us and seeming to wonder. "Only *Gringos* would be foolish enough to do such a thing when you can take a car." But the feeling was coming to us: We are covering distance; we are on our way; the adventure has begun.

That day is one which I remember especially well. The thinning trees off toward the haze shrouded horizon appeared like the tips of rounded icebergs rising gracefully from a yellow prairie sea. The day was completely peaceful, with nothing stirring; sounds of cicadas and cattle and heat, muted by distance, rose unimpeded to be dissipated in the all-absorbing vastness of the sky, or if a slight breeze stirred, to be carried lazily in one direction so that down wind you could hear an easy conversation, but upwind you were deaf to the most fervent call. But then it was calm, and the heat rose in billows from the plain and among the grazing, swishing cattle who were crowded into the muddy stagnant pools to drink and find relief from the oppressive insects.

At last we could see a giant mechanical sprinkler, looking like a walking suspension bridge as it circled a field and rained its cool mist in a great swath. Tall enough for one to ride a horse under and stand in the saddle, it chugged and hiccupped driven by the power of a big V-8 engine. Seeking its relief we walked beneath, having drunk our fill at the spigot, and we saturated our clothes until they were stinging cold when they touched our skin. And yet because of the heat they were well on their way to being dry by the time we returned to our horses. For a few minutes our thirst was satiated, and we reveled in luxurious moist comfort, defying the searing countryside around us. It could afford our brief escape, for we would soon enough return to its searing grasp, and it would begin again to work its inexorable offices upon us. But now the relief was too delicious to concern ourselves with anything else. And we drank as we had never drunk before and poured the water over ourselves as we did. No Moor, lounging in his shaded Spanish garden, was ever more appreciative of the qualities of water. Its presence was as dominating as a wood fire in a snowbound mountain cabin, and it had no less fascination than had it been a whole ocean before us instead of a running faucet and a long, rainbow-pierced drizzle.

We rode on into the afternoon, down into the grassy bottom and up the thistle-choked ravine onto the sandy hills beside it. Towards evening we crossed to the south side of the river and rode about a mile into the undulating hills towards a windmill where we were to make camp. We unloaded the horses and hobbled them for their night of grazing. Then we collected wood for our campfire and cooked our dinner. As we lay down to sleep on the crest of a gently sloping hill affording us a fine view, we were surrounded by grass taller than our heads, as though we were cupped in the fur hands of the great prairie. Overhead a myriad of stars shown; no other light was visible in any direction. Resting our heads on our saddles we sank into an uninterrupted swoon, out of a consciousness of the world and into the sleep of fantasy and peace.

The next morning began a ritual ordeal which was to be the bane of our coexistence with our horses for fully half the trip. We had hobbled each of the horses with leather straps between their two front feet and tied a long lead rope to each halter so that we could get near enough to catch them even should they exhibit any wariness. We did not want to chance being left out on the open plains to carry saddle and equipment without horses, and we did not know how they were going to act when given even a shackled form of freedom. Usually they would stay around camp and graze close by before sleeping, then in the morning, graze again for a while, and finally, after an hour or so of daylight, move off. Before going to sleep we had heard them nearby, chewing and hopping their hobbled gait from stand to stand. But this morning when we awoke there were no horses to be found and our big bell was one of the things we'd left in the truck. We had no idea which direction they had gone nor even how large was the pasture in which we were camped, for even with our binoculars we could only see two fences; the one behind us and the adjacent one we had crossed to get in. To make matters worse, the leather on the new hobbles had stretched, and we found one lying in the grass near the camp. So began our frustrating search which was to delay our departure until the heat of the summer day began to build to an enervating level. It was a search which was to be repeated a number of times until we were finally to realize that the horses always headed for the last gate through which they came—a tendency that lasted the whole trip. They were always returning to Kansas, the point of departure, and I have no doubt that had we given them unrestricted freedom they would have ultimately returned, like some prairie Lassie, to Wagon Bed Springs. Jack headed south and I headed east, and watching for rattlesnakes as we went, began a wide swinging search. After an hour we came over a small hill and saw them congregated up against the fence, about as far as where we had crossed the river. Two of the hobbles were off and Red's movements alone had been restricted by the lead rope wrapping around his hobble, which restricted him to a short, bowed hop. We never did find the other hobble and were thereafter forced to hobble the pack horse, using her as a bell mare to attract the others. Following are some of my notes which indicate our belabored progress:

"Sunday, July 9

"After a frustrating beginning today, we rode along the north side of the river. The trees are getting denser, although not too thick to ride among. We crossed a dirt road by some cattle pens and elaborately-constructed water tanks. The bank on the north side is at times very precipitous and forces us up out of the river onto high ground. No sign of the wagon tracks after the morning crossing. We nooned on an island in the river where the horses could graze among the Tamarisk and willows. We managed to get under some bushes for shade and after a fantastic lunch of tuna salad sandwiches, we dozed a while even as we tried to keep an eye on the horses. In the oppressive heat a chance to sit in the shade and eat a really good sandwich with the crunchy feel of celery is a glorious luxury. It's amazing how a meal can revive one's spirits. After lunch we resaddled the horses, loaded the pack horse, and crossed the river. I was climbing a steep bank about fifty feet high and leading the pack horse. Behind me, Jack was crossing the river when suddenly Linda sank up to her belly in the sand. Jack started to get off and she struggled up to the surface. She has small feet and with his weight cannot cross safely where Red and I can. We had been looking out for quicksand and Jack had been following my tracks. He was quite shaken by the whole thing. We rode up to some high rolling hills on the north side of the river. It was grassy and we were able to see the tracks descending the hill to the west. From our vantage point we could see for miles both in front of us and behind. In the foreground, clouds were moving rapidly to the east from which we had come, giving the earth a dappled light and shadow effect. With the great distance ahead that we were able to see, it provided a very spectacular sight.

"Turtles continue to appear, leaving their curious tracks as a reminder of their passing. This afternoon we rode into a good site by the river with water tanks and big trees rather free of undergrowth. Several wild turkeys flew into the woods at our arrival and we very soon used the water to drink and pour all over ourselves for refreshment. I found that a bandana which I can wet and put over my head or around my neck is the most refreshing article of clothing in my current wardrobe. We rode through the bottom land stumbling into numerous fences and some French breeder cattle which were very curious about us. So far we have had no trouble with fences, almost invariably hitting the fence right where the gate is located and frequently these are open. Again we crossed to the south bank and rode up into the hills near a water tank. High up and clear of the trees we get a beautiful open view, a little windy, and the ground is poor: sand with sage and clumps of grass, and it is there that we tie the horses until dark when we hobble them. Tonight we use the small tent as it looks like rain."

According to his observations of the stars, Sibley passed through here in 1825, having said this of the area:

"Friday, 30th September

"We started from this miserable spot at sunrise, the morning very pleasant and fair. Steered South 47 W. out upon high level prairie, and at the distance of 3 miles from camp came to a pond of pretty good water, where the grass was also pretty good, here we halted to get breakfast. At 45 minutes past 10 we cont'd our route over the high level plain 8 miles and then turned into the left So. 10 east to the creek which we struck in a large valley, affording plenty of good grass and running water. Dug in the sand about 18 inches deep and got pretty good water, that which stands or runs on the surface is sulpherous and brackish and strongly seasoned with Buffalo urine. Before we left this place, Mr. B. took the latitude by and observation of Rigel and fixes it as 37°-14'17"."[20] (About 12 miles northeast of Rolla, Kansas.)

And Josiah Gregg's party was plagued by curious camp followers as it journeyed through here in 1831.

"On the following day we had been in motion but a few minutes when the Indians began flocking around us in large numbers, and by the time we encamped in the evening we had perhaps a thousand of these pertinacious creatures, males and females of all ages and descriptions, about us. At night every means, without resorting to violence, was employed to drive them away, but without entire success. At this time a small band of warriors took the round of our camp, and serenaded us with a monotonous song of hee-o-ehes, with the view, I suppose, of gaining permission to remain; hoping, no doubt, to be able to drive a fair business at pilfering during the night. In fact, a few small articles were already missing, and it was now discovered that they had purloined a pig of lead (between fifty and a hundred pounds weight) from one of the cannon-carriages where it had been carelessly left. This increased the uneasiness which already prevailed to a considerable extent; and many of us would imagine it already moulded into bullets, which we were perhaps destined to receive before morning from the muzzles of their fusils. Some were even so liberal as to express a willingness to pardon the theft rather than give the Indians the trouble of sending it back in so hasty a manner. After a tedious night of suspense and conjecture it was no small relief to those whose feelings had been so highly wrought upon to find, on waking up in the morning, that every man still retained his scalp.

"We started at a much earlier hour this morning, in hopes to leave our Indian tormentors behind; but they were too wide awake for us. By the time the wagoners had completed the task of gearing their teams, the squaws had geared their dogs and loaded them with their lodge poles and covers and other light plunder and were traveling fast in our wake. Much to our comfort, however, the greatest portion abandoned us before night; but the next day several of the chiefs overtook us again at noon, seeming anxious to renew the treaty of peace. The truth is, the former treaty had never been sealed—they had received no presents, which form an indispensable ratification of all their treaties with the whites. Some fifty or sixty dollars' worth of goods having been made up for them, they now left us, apparently satisfied; and although they continued to return and annoy us for a couple of days longer, they at last entirely disappeared.

"It was generally supposed at the time that there was a great number of Comanches and Arapahoes among this troop of savages; but they were principally if not altogether Blackfeet and Gros Ventres. We afterward learned that on their return to the northern mountains they met with a terrible defeat from the Sioux and other neighboring tribes, in which they were said to have lost more than half their number. We now encountered a great deal of wet weather; in fact this region is famous for cold protracted rains of two or three days' duration. Storms of hailstones larger than hen's eggs are not uncommon, frequently accompanied by the most tremendous hurricanes. The violence of the wind is sometimes so great that, as I have heard, two road-wagons were once capsized by one of these terrible thunder-gusts; the rain at the same time flooding the plain to the depth of several inches. In short, I doubt if there is any known region out of the tropics that can head the great prairies in getting up thunder-storms combining so many of the elements of the awful and sublime.

"During these storms the guards were often very careless. This was emphatically the case with us, notwithstanding our knowledge of the proximity of a horde of savages. In fact, the caravan was subject to so little control that the patience of Capt. Stanley underwent some very severe trials; so much so that he threatened more than once to resign. Truly, there is not a better school for testing a man's temper than the command of a promiscuous caravan of independent traders. The rank of captain is, of course, but little more than nominal. Every proprietor of a two horse wagon is apt to assume as much authority as the commander himself, and to issue his orders without the least consultation at headquarters. It is easy, then, to conceive that the captain has anything but an enviable berth. He is expected to keep order while few are disposed to obey—loaded with execrations for every mishap, whether accidental or otherwise; and when he attempts to remonstrate he only renders himself ridiculous, being entirely without power to enforce his commands. It is to be regretted that some system of maritime law has not been introduced among these traders to secure subordination, which can never be attained while the commander is invested with no legal authority. For my own part, I can see no reason why the captain of a prairie caravan should not have as much power to call his men to account for disobedience or mutiny as the captain of a ship upon the high sea."[21]

Monday, July 10

We awoke this morning to find a beautiful day but no sign of the horses. This is really worrisome because we can see several miles in all directions but south and there is no sign of them. It is going to be hot soon and loading them on this bare, exposed hillside is going to be exhausting. Through the binoculars we located them in the trees back by the river and about two miles east. No wood so we have to cook with dead sage roots and cow chips. A pretty lousy fire but at least it can cook the powdered eggs, which are more terrible than the fire. While I cook and pack up camp, Jack goes after the horses. This morning we cross the Rolla road and there is a historical marker:

Santa Fe Trail, 1822-1872
Marked by the Daughters of the American Revolution and the State of Kansas, 1906

As close as we get to Rolla, Kansas

There's no real sign of the Trail and I am beginning to feel lost. It's hotter than hell and no matter how much we drink we are always thirsty. From high on the prairie we can see the town of Rolla opposite us. Jack wants to ride in and get some cold beer, which sounds fantastic, but the town looks like it's ten miles away and that's a full day's ride for us 'round trip. What about going back to the road and hitchhiking? Too much time to spend. We can kill a half day at every crossing if we start that habit. But we've gotten the idea into our heads, dammit, so we decide to ride over to a ranch house about a mile off and see if we can buy some. When we get there, it's abandoned. Well, there's another, we'll try it. No luck! By now we're in the Cimarron National Grasslands and they're doing some fancy soil punching to capture rainfall. It's hell to walk on and there's no sign of the Trail.

Late in the afternoon we come to the Wilberton crossing, and there's huge black clouds all over the sky. A great rain cloud is moving over the river with an enormous gray wall sloping between it and the ground. We're dead tired and so get off to wait out the storm and have a smoke. It's windy and sandy and cold as we huddle against a sand hill where we spook out a large snake at home in his domain. A little rain falls on us and then gives up. The sun is low and there's an eerie yellow light on the ground turning the grass to a dark orange-green color almost vibrant between the black and zinc-white clouds above and the warm descending sun ahead. And then I begin to discern it. At first a faint disturbance in the surface ecology, a fragmentary line of tumbleweed growing in a wide arch towards the river. Of course! Because of the heavy vegetation and lessened erosion the Trail is not the obvious set of ruts which we were used to, and we have been unable to recognize the signs. It reminds me of the *Camino Real* in the *Jornada* towards El Paso, just a higher rate of thistle and other weeds defining more of a direction than a path. It's like finding an old friend, I no longer feel lost; I'm surprised at how much the Trail has come to provide meaning in our lives. When we are near it, our action seems more decisive and clear. When we can't find it, we're more listless and uncertain. But now we are back on its course again.

We follow it several miles quite close to the river. At dusk the tracks, which have become smoothly grassed depressions made obvious by the angle of the sun, turn in towards the river. The bank is about nine feet high here, although it was probably lower in frontier days judging by the width of the cuts into the side which give access into the river. What does it mean? Obviously, the banks had to be cut to make a gradual slope so that the wagons could get down. The river is grassy on this side and lined with trees, and I count sixteen cuts in the bank, one after the other, with worn grooves leading to them. They're strung out for a distance of several hundred yards. Fantastic! This must have been a crossing, a campground or a place to water oxen. The parallel fanning of the ruts indicates the first wagons probably went to one end and the others pulled off behind, further down river as they arrived. Too much! Suddenly I feel transported back into history, as though the wagons had just left or could arrive at any moment. We are stopping in the middle of an historic camping ground with all the evidence of its past use. We can feel the impact of the Trail as a living, working thing around us.

We set up camp under a big cottonwood tree in the river bottom below the furthest cut. I go check the river to see if it is likely to rise to a point where we might wake up as driftwood. The river is flowing high and muddy but a considerable distance away with a string of banks between us. But there is trash piled four feet high against the trees where we are from previous floods. I don't know. Jack wants to stay right there, so I

Bank cuts lead to campsites

agree and we cook supper and eat. We feel great about rediscovering the Trail—it's like having an old friend back. So we break out some Start and Grain and lemon for a little R&R.

    The horses are hobbled, but we go up to check on them after dark and look again at our discovery and discuss it with the horses. In the exuberance of the event I decide to frolic with Red. I sidle up next to him and next thing he knows I've jumped on his back and I'm hanging onto his mane and I'm hollerin' like a Comanche! This brings his usual response and suddenly I find out how he manages to get halfway home every night with his hobbles on. One minute I'm on top of him jumpin' around and he's surprised, the next minute he's in a dead run from standing still and I am the surprised one. If I hadn't known he was hobbled to start with, I would never have guessed. I've never seen him go any faster, the only difference is that his run is half jump and has the action of a pile driver. After a short distance I decide I've had enough of this ride, and I'd better vacate while the choice is mine. So down I come with a bounce and a running start perpetuating the motion of his buck from the ground. That night Red and I come to another one of our understandings of just

Checking the horses before dark

what the other is about, at least I learned something about him. And I can't say it wasn't fun.

The next morning we bask in the luxury of our tree-canopied camp and eat a magnificent breakfast of cheese omelette, toast, sweets and coffee, punctuated by delicious relaxation with a cigar. In this true bliss nothing can stir me to unpleasant thoughts or undesired efforts but for the fact that when we casually struggle to our feet to check the horses, they've gone!

One minute Jeanie is standing at the top of the bank looking down at us and the next minute they are all gone. Jesus Christ. Those goddam horses; I'd just as soon shoot the s.o.b.s as look at them at a time like this. Goddamit, can't even relax around this place without having to get up and do useless work that doesn't prove a friggin' thing. What are you knot headed bastards trying to prove?

Way over there about a mile, just passing the water tank and headin' east, they're shuffling out of sight. I take a bridle and a towel and when they see me coming they stop. Well I'll take the opportunity to bathe in the scummy brown water and then mount Red and lead the others back. Of course, they can't miss the chance to botch things up further by crossing back and forth and tangling up their ropes, walking too slow or too fast so that I'm dropping my towel and my clothes are falling on the ground, and I have no saddle to tie the lead rope around the horn (they're probably waiting for me to tie it around my neck) so one of them slips out of my hand. Oh, the hell with it, I'll let Linda walk home by herself, I've had enough of this horror show!!

That day we rode along a dirt road which followed the ruts. In the morning we passed a line rider's shack and asked directions of the wife who was at home. She seemed somewhat surprised to have two weatherbeaten men on horseback ride up in that desolate place, and we found ourselves prolonging the conversation just to hear the sound of someone else's voice. It was then we realized that we were beginning to get lonely. It was not even the fact that here was a woman, because surprisingly enough, our exertions in our daily routine were so exhausting that being away from the opposite sex was not even significant. It was just that not seeing a single other person for many days was making us miss human contact and desire to be around our own species. It was not a feeling I can remember experiencing before, a sort of delicate stirring, a feeling of rapport, companionship, and welcome between people just because we were people and shared living. It was a source of profound pleasure which I wish I could remember to cultivate under other circumstances.

And so we rode on that day in the easiest and most memorable mood of well-being. The road made it easy for the horses and they were alert and energetic; the country was unspoiled, looking as it must have when man first saw it, a little greener perhaps, but open, rolling, and divided by a wide ribbon of large cottonwood and willow trees. Apparently people had tried to farm the area in the twenties, but the dust bowl had blown them away. We later heard about a house beside the river which was completely buried by blowing dust so that people had to dig down to reach the chimney. But now it looked like virgin grassland with no sign of human activity except windmills and the small pump houses of the huge Hugoton gas field. Shortly after noon we crossed the Elkhart highway a little east of middle spring and Point of Rocks (Kansas). Now was our chance to get some cold beer!

We stashed our equipment in the trees, tied the horses where they could graze, and caught a ride with a passing truck into the town of Elkhart. It was the first civilization we had seen in four days, but somehow it seemed more like four weeks. It felt good just to sit in a chair: a perfect height from the ground, just the right support for the back, ah, what luxury! And that first cold glass of beer. One is divine, a cold effervescent quenching of previously unrelieved thirst, two are still good but it's diminishing: if you want to maximize the joy quit there. On the street we learn that it's 110° that day. No wonder we can't work in the sun. On television (imagine, color television and electric refrigerators) the Democratic convention is going on; no one is interested. I guess Kansas is the Republican version of the Deep South. The side streets are neat and tree-lined; the kids cruise the downtown boulevards in their souped-up cars. It's a prosperous and pleasant setting—one of those Midwestern towns out of the movies of the fifties and novels of the twenties: under the billowing cumulus clouds of the prairie, first a huge grain elevator, white like a marble monument, then a shady village full of good, open-faced people, warm, reassuring, and stifling to the young. But a welcomed oasis from the harsh elements of the natural setting on which it floats. Rides are easy to catch; we discuss the Trail with the interested driver, and hear some of the local lore. Thanks for the ride.

We camp at Point of Rock, a cliff overlooking the river and the highest point in southwest Kansas. It is barren and windswept but affords a good view of the surrounding country. The Indians used it as a lookout. The river has shifted considerably to the north, closer to the rock, since the days of the Trail. Below the cliff and directly on the bank is the foundation of the house and an out building of the former Point of Rocks Ranch. A flood in 1914 caused the river to cut north and wash out the buildings in the night, drowning the rancher's wife and two daughters. It must have been a terrible scene, and looking down on it I can imagine a dark, rainy night. Mrs. Bright was probably waiting for her husband to come home out of the storm; wondering what the capricious river is doing out there in all the fury. She tries to pretend everything is normal and put the girls to bed so that they won't worry; sitting in the kerosene light listening to the storm outside. Then . . . "What's that noise?"

The Cimarron roars closer, water pounding and trees crashing their way downstream. Then the south wall begins to move and the floor rises and sinks. With a shudder, the wall falls out into the surging water and is gone. For an instant, she is looking out into the night and the fury of the storm, like looking into the horrifying jaws of hell itself. She is too paralyzed to move at first, the light blows out and things begin to fly around the room, hitting her in the face as she struggles back into presence of mind.

"Got to get to the kids and get them out." She is groping against the north wall, feeling for the door knob. She finds it and the door begins to open just as a great tearing sound wrenches the house loose from its clinging hillside and tosses it into grisly oblivion.

"Oh, my babies."

The next morning the people search the debris and bury them where they are found, five miles downstream.

> Sweet sleep, embrace them
> For they can ne'er be free
> From terror of that night time's
> Memory.

The rancher leaves his broken life behind and settles in Colorado.

Other struggles of life and death occurred here which add memories and significance to this place: A pursuit through the snow one night by traders who are afraid of making noises which might attract Indians as they hunt for their escaped livestock. In their underwear and lacking boots they carelessly risk their lives and obtain more fortunate results than one is used to hearing recalled in the annals of the Trail. In 1846 a young soldier from Philadelphia was bitten by a tarantula and buried at the foot of the cliff. Today there is no sign of his grave. East of the mesa about 3/4 mile is Middle Cimarron Spring. It had disappeared in the dust storms of the 1950s and was reestablished by constructing a small dam on the arroyo. In the old days, the river was usually dry. What surface water there was was alkaline and had a cathartic effect on men and animals alike, seriously weakening them for their travel exertions. Better water could usually be found by digging, but in this dry, sandy country, springs like the Lower, Middle, and Upper were landmarks viewed as oases of rest and refreshment in what seemed a parched desert. Here Sibley camped with his surveying party of 1825 on October 2.

At this point, my notes (Wednesday, July 12) indicate some improvement in our general condition.

> "We are now five days out and have recovered enough from the physical shock of our new regime to have some surplus of energy. Before now it was a struggle just to do the simplest requirements and there was

Middle Springs, Kansas

Middle Springs with duck flying

no energy left to write, to be interested in the history of the sites we passed, or to be of more than spare humor. Now I am beginning to feel my body respond to food and rest and to be capable of occasional displays of gaiety in mood. It is still very tiring because of the heat which is oppressive. Again, the horses got away this morning and crossed to a fence almost a mile away. We had one horse left and Jack rode it for an hour and a half searching for the others. Initially, he took off for the north, where he thought he saw them by a cattle tank. After breaking camp, I began to follow his progress through the binoculars. I could see that he had pursued a herd of cattle, and I soon found the horses due east. I fired the gun to signal him that he was going the wrong way but he was unable to hear. I had to climb over the cliff to wait in the shade of a niche, out of the heat.

"From the top of the mesa last night we were able to clearly see the lights of Elkhart, 8 miles south, and to the west a tower of lights which we could not identify. We rode west from the mesa over the gas field road which was just hard-packed sand surrounded by wretched brush and throbbing gas pumps. It is so hot that I can't stand to ride in the middle of the road because the reflecting sand increases the heat by twenty to thirty degrees and the light blinds my eyes. The horses are becoming jaded and will barely plod along. I am leading the pack horse who drags so much that I must wrap the lead rope around the pummel of my saddle and literally pull her down the Trail. The deer flies and other insects swarm around us and the horses. Their bites are so severe that they raise a welt which can itch for days. Occasionally a cicada rises before us with a hissing that keeps us aware of snakes. The horses swish their tails and nod their heads up and down to shake the flies off. When some land on Red he practically stops his forward movement and begins to shake and snap to free himself of the plague. It is impossible for me to take my shirt off because of the insects' bites. I spend the day looking Red over for flies so he can bear to travel. They generally land on his neck and are easy to reach, but sometimes they get on his belly where I can't see and then the only way I know of them is from his conduct. After a while they catch on to my killing game and start hiding under the protection of his mane, and I spend the next few hours randomly slapping at his neck and sweeping up his mane with my hand to discourage them. The poor beast is suffering to distraction, but our arrangement improves things considerably. Bugs are so thick that at times I kill three or four with one slap while others feast on an adjacent area. The sun continues to be strong and I have no doubts we would die in this region if we were out here without straw hats. It amazes me to see how much protection from the dizzying light and the searing heat is provided by my hat. It is the closest thing to having a tree and a roof with me at all times, and if I had no other clothes on, I would prefer the sunburn and the bites to prompt sunstroke which would follow upon the hat's loss. When I lie on the ground, having my hat over my face provides a relief of many degrees temperature and allows the fantasy of escape from this burning and barren inferno. This has got to be the most godforsaken place on the whole Trail. Even the vegetation is an insult to human sensitivities. It is hotter than yesterday.

"Sometime today we will cross into Colorado and go from central time to mountain time, gaining an hour. Then tomorrow we will go back into central time, no big deal when you are walking one mile an hour! At midday we unpack the horses in the shade of a great spreading cottonwood tree and fix ourselves a hearty lunch. In spite of the heat, we are always hungry when tired, and a good lunch does as much to revive our languid spirits as it does for our strength. After lunch we lie in the shade and listen to the buzzing of the insects. I climb the cottonwood tree to see what kind of view it affords. Looking out from the leaves of a thick and gnarled branch, I can tell what it is that kids appreciate in a tree house: the secure feeling of a secret place with strong comforting arms enveloping them in protective safety."

Riding on into Colorado, the country is sand hills and sage and sorry footing. In the '30s this was all blowing, drifting sand. Today another generation of abandoned farm houses testifies to the depopulation of the countryside. Gas and oil wells provide some roads and the temperature is in the 100s. Just surviving is my main effort and right now I could not care less that this is the Santa Fe Trail or how many thousands of people came by here. Under these conditions one has little appreciation of history. We cross the Texas Trail, a twelve-mile-wide "National Road," from the Panhandle to the tick-free open ranges of Montana, Wyoming and the Dakotas. Right now it rates only an apathetic glance. We're looking for water and all of the windmills are shut off.

Sometime in the afternoon we ride up to a once elegant but now deserted farm house which possessed a porch and bay windows; one of its inheritors, a huge owl, flies out of the old living room. Tall weeds grow in the yard and varmint tunnels undermine the foundation. Behind is a pond of water and a stock tank. The tank is green and stagnant with a large, dead frog floating in it and another sharing his last days with the corpse. The horses sniff the water and turn away. We ride over to another tank and climb the windmill to turn it by hand and draw water, but it's useless. We return to the corral and the horses drink from the puddle. We can resist that temptation. Remounting we ride down the road through the still green tumbleweeds, among the darting lizards and rasping cicadas which fly up before us and bounce off of our bodies. I am in the lead and Jack is leading Jeanie. Suddenly, on the ground before me, a large snake slithers ahead. About the time I see the rattles, I call to Jack "rattlesnake" and pull Red to the side. The snake coils practically beneath Red's front feet as we dodge to the side. I grab at the scabbard for my rifle. Red, who was unaware or indifferent to the snake until now, catches my excitement and is swept by fear. As I try to dismount, he starts bucking and I am barely able to get the gun. A shot through the back and the snake begins to twist and roll. Red is twisting and circling at my side. Another shot and the snake is dead. To make sure we step on his neck and cut off his head. He is a big one, measuring several feet, and as we skin him out he continues to writhe and coil about my arm so that I occasionally steal a glance at the head lying over there just to convince myself that he's really dead. We salt the skin and tie it on the pack saddle, packing the meat in a sack. It's getting late and we had better find a camp with some water before dark or well spend a pretty uncomfortable night.

We push ahead, riding up a draw about a half mile from the river, which is now just about at our level, having only low banks instead of the cliffs of before.

Jack rides ahead to find a camp while I lead Jeanie. At dusk we find a windmill near a small hill which gives us a view of the faint silhouette of Point of Rocks to the east and the lighted derrick which looks like a small feedlot tower in the river bottom ahead. We unpack the horses and set up the tent just as it's getting dark.

Red and Linda are down at the tank drinking and eating the grass in the swampy overflow of the tank. Jeanie is too tired to move and stands framed against the twilighted sky near by us. Suddenly, around the hill, some two or three hundred yards beyond us and towards the river, a pack of a half dozen coyotes set up a fearsome racket of shrieking and howling. Jeanie jumps and is soon trotting down the hill to join the protection of the other horses.

The evening is gorgeous. The late, golden twilight reminds me of fall in the mountain country of Colorado (strong light and purple hills). The rich, burning sunlight creates shadows by every clump of grass, giving the earth a depth of colored light and shadow which causes the landscape to vibrate with vitality. Then, the bright, glowing afterlight provides strong, red contrast to the even shade of the gently rolling hills and the winding tree-lined river bottom, the brilliant red and orange shining horizon, and ultimately the deepening dark blueness of the overhead sky. In places the great stacks of feather pillows, which are the Kansas clouds, present their multi-tiered panorama of light: brilliant white and cadmium yellow in the afternoon, dissolving into red and orange and pink in the last daylight. The sky is still bright and clear, but the earth is in shadow. First, the detail of the ground is lost. Game emerges from daytime hiding into the dusk, almost undistinguishable from the dabs of dark detail which are the landmarks giving background. The ground darkens but the sky seems so bright that we still expect to be able to see and are surprised when we cannot find some item, or stumble on a log in the obscurity, fooled by the illusion of lingering vision.

Around us the coyotes are closer than they've ever come, prowling, whining their plaintive bark, and giving a simultaneous sense of nature's comforting presence as well as danger. The effect is mixed into the kind of exciting medley I find in Rousseau's *Sleeping Gypsy*. A blend of thrill and of repose which results in a moment of dramatic tension.

We lay our saddles on a log opposite the fire and soon have a cozy little camp. We enjoy a drink of Grain and Start as our fire crackles beneath a kettle of boiling onion, potato, pepper and rattlesnake. People say that snake tastes like chicken, but judging from the size of this one, he was old—he tastes more like a rangy rooster. The meat is rich and heavy and very filling—pure protein, says Jack. We are soon full and stretch out beneath the most beautiful star-laden sky. The melodies of a harmonica swirl on the breeze in our camp, and we speculate about living and joy and the past. Then, with all quiet but the prolonged serenade of the nearby coyotes, we drift into welcomed, restful sleep.

The next day was more of the same. Jack had been conducting a heated argument with Linda as to how much and how long she would carry. She would reach back and try to take a nip out of him and he would slap her on the neck so she'd jump. Then, finally, I had heard a yell and she shot sideways about three feet, indicating she had gotten in a good bite; he was rolling around in agony rubbing his shin. Soon, it started to swell and pain his leg until it was hard for him to mount his horse. Then, to add injury to insult, he had begun to get gout in the same leg. This had been going on a couple of days and by now it was all beginning to take a toll on his mobility and humor. We encountered more of the same weather and conditions, passed an oil drill at noon (the lights we had been seeing), encountered some red deer along the river, and by late afternoon reached the famous Willow Bar crossing. Here the Trail leaves the Cimarron and enters what used to be the most dangerous Indian country, known as "no man's land." It was as far as we were to make it with our pack horse. We had been on the road six days and had covered the first 62 miles averaging 10 miles a day; now we were to leave the river and cross the high, barren plains of the Oklahoma panhandle.

Willow Bar Crossing, 1935 *(Denver Public Library)*

5 ∞ The High Lonesome

Looking back on what we experienced during daily travel, I am struck by my inability to communicate what the series of experiences did to us, the kinds of feelings I had under the strain of circumstances, and the frustration of mistakes which characterized those initial days. At the time I recall being so completely absorbed in the experience that all my efforts and thoughts went into the daily requirements of living and achieving some meager comfort. And at the time it seemed as though that experience was the only one which was real to me; the only one which had ever existed for me. I was so immersed in the perspective of that situation that I could not conceive of any other way of being. It was similar to the perspective associated with intense pain: when it is occurring, it is impossible to remember what life was like without it. The heat, the work, the countryside, the slow passage of time, and the basic requirements of survival were all that I could imagine life as being made up of, so all-absorbing was that effort.

Now as I look back on it, it is almost equally difficult for me to recover that perspective. The effort of catching and saddling my horse in the searing heat and then riding all day to cover a mere 10 miles left me with a new sense of personal economy. I became aware of the tremendous effort required to accomplish the simplest routine. Against so harsh a surrounding, human and animal energy seemed overwhelmingly feeble. The process of living was like pouring our energy into a funnel; we'd put everything we had into one end, and a small, physical accomplishment would dribble out of the other. And all the time circumstances were lurking to undermine our efforts. If we were careless about putting food away, an animal would steal it. If we did not secure a knot with extra surveillance, something would be lost. If we were too tired to organize camp before sleeping, a surprise rain would come and something would be ruined.

In the early days these things were a special problem, either due to our ignorance or to our exhausted state. As we built our strength, events were not so debilitating. I found over time a new awareness of my body, which I had not experienced before. I came to know both my capabilities, and those of my horse, to meet various situations.

Most striking was the relation between my food intake and my energy level. Once a spare habitual routine was established, I became aware of the close relationship between my appetite and my capability (and willingness) for work. Skipping a meal, which I can do with no awareness of consequences in civilization, was out of the question here. The degree of appetite varied widely, but I was always clear as to exactly how much I wanted to eat. Sometimes a light breakfast and sometimes a large one was needed. And, in spite of the heat, I generally ate quite a bit without feeling full or uncomfortable, even when trotting for hours afterwards. My emotional state was also governed by my diet. Feelings of exhaustion accompanied by hunger led to depression, while physical exhaustion alone would give rise to a relaxed sense of tiredness. Food was always a source of recovered energy and uplifted spirits and so became the central item in our sparse culture. It was much the same with sleep; there was never any distraction from our tired condition, and so we always responded immediately to our body's call to cease. We would awaken the next day completely severed from those feelings of limitation experienced the previous evening.

And yet, in spite of what seemed then to be difficulties, both with our gear and between ourselves, I had a strong feeling of completeness in the duties of the daily life, and a feeling of wellbeing towards my role in these endeavors. I had the sense of possessing everything we needed and that I could just continue to do this forever. Our sense of purpose was provided by the Trail; and when we lost it, there was a feeling of not only being lost but also of being meaningless. There were almost no houses along the Trail, and those there were were usually abandoned. The fact that it all seemed so unchanged gave us a strong sense of continuity with history, and with what had once been a major thrust of the developing nation. And, personally, our lives seemed uncomplicated and satisfying, and our purposes though limited, unusually clear. We could not call what we were doing fun; indeed, it was some of the hardest physical work I had ever done; but it was good effort, with moments of pleasure, and even our mistakes could be worked out physically so that they did not create stresses and tensions which remained to cloud our emotions. At the end of the day we were simply exhausted, and nothing else mattered. Nothing was accumulated but the miles and our gradually increasing strength. It makes me wonder what we, as a people, have given up by leaving the physical life behind. The benefits of great energy resources have not been attended by meaningful ideals giving direction for their use, nor with a sense of achievement and reward for personal participation. For between what we are capable of doing in a civilization and what we were capable of accomplishing in that situation is a fantastic gulf, as great as the difference between abundance and subsistence, between energetic health and chronic illness. And yet, in spite of the material luxury of modern life compared to the incredible hardships of the past, the emotional benefits for many people seem to be a net loss. Certainly, I can understand why many people want to cling to the land in preference to the occupations of interpersonal manipulation and petty aggrandizement.

I came to enjoy the simplest pleasures, like arriving in camp at the end of the day and taking off my boots. After days of sleeping on the ground, to lie on a foam mattress for a night was the maximum joy. On the other hand, our bodies developed a certain discipline so that a bed was too soft, and I could not sleep comfortably in one for a week after arriving home. And, of course, there were the pleasures of the outdoors and of companionship. The excitement of encountering persons along the way. Occasionally inhospitable, defensive, and withdrawn; usually intelligent, cordial, and sharing. These things provided the quality of life which we came to appreciate as a source of physical and emotional satisfaction and of learning about ourselves.

Eventually, I acquired such a novel awareness that I became apprehensive about returning to civilization and its diversions. But by now we had reached a state of preparedness which made us less vulnerable to the physical exhaustion which had been so large a part of our experience so far. Soon the weather would cloud up and become decidedly cooler, and we would leave the tangled river bottom for the endless openness of the grama-grassed plains.

Willow Bar Crossing is located on a long, gentle bend in the river. The crossing began above the present highway bridge, near an old washed-out road whose access is lined with trees like an approach to some deserted plantation. The Bar is gone but aerial photos show that the crossing went into the river and upstream a little before coming out on the other side. The south side was flat in those days, but since the dust bowl of the '30s, has been silted into broken, sandy hills which serve as prelude to the gradual rise out of the Cimarron Valley onto the barren plateau which is the new course of the Trail. Entering the crossing from the northeast, the path through the green bottomland is marked by occasional weeds and ruts. But in places more recent meanders have sliced off sections of bank leaving one hanging at the edge of some minor precipice as he tries to follow the course. This most famous of crossings between the Arkansas and the Canadian is the setting of many a harrowing tale. The Indians would wait for wagon trains to reach midriver where teamsters would be preoccupied and relatively defenseless and then would sweep down on them to fight with the best advantage. It was near here that Colonel Vizcarra nearly met death at the hands of the Gros Ventres in 1829, and the preceding year the burial of McNees and Monroe had culminated in revenge against some Indians that precipitated major Indian harassment of traffic on the Trail.

Gregg relates his experience here in 1831:

"After following the course of the Cimarron for two days longer we at length reached a place called Willow Bar, where we took the usual midday respite of two or three hours, to afford the animals time to feed and our cooks to prepare dinner. Our wagons were regularly formed, and the animals turned loose to graze at leisure, with only a day-guard to watch them. Those who had finished their dinners lay stretched upon their blankets and were just beginning to enjoy the luxury of a siesta, when all of a sudden the fearful and oft-reiterated cry of 'Indians!' turned this scene of repose into one of bustle and confusion.

"From the opposite ridge, at the distance of a mile, a swarm of savages were seen coming upon us at full charge, and their hideous whoop and yell soon resounded through the valley. Such a jumbling of promiscuous voices I never expect to hear again. Every one fancied himself a commander and vociferated his orders accordingly. The air was absolutely rent with the cries of 'Let's charge 'em, boys'—'Fire upon 'em, boys!' 'Reserve, don't fire till they come nearer'—while the voice of our captain was scarcely distinguishable in his attempts to prevent such rash proceedings. As the prairie Indians often approach their friends as well as enemies in this way, Captain Stanley was unwilling to proceed to extremities lest they might be peacefully inclined. But a popping salute and the whizzing of fusil balls over our heads soon explained their intentions. We returned them several rifle shots by way of compliment, but without effect, as they were at too great a distance.

"A dozen cannoneers now surrounded our artillery, which was charged with canister. Each of them had, of course, something to say. 'Elevate her; she'll ground,' one would suggest. 'She'll over-shoot, now,' rejoined another. At last, after raising and lowering the six pounder several times, during which process the Indians had time to retreat beyond reach of shot, the match was finally applied and—bang' went the gun, but the charge grounded midway. This was followed by two or three shots with single ball, but apparently without effect; although there were some with sharp eyes who fancied they saw Indians or horses wounded at every fire. We came off equally unscathed from the conflict, barring a horse of but little value which ran away and was taken by the enemy. The Indians were about a hundred in number and supposed to be Comanches, though they might have been a band of warriors belonging to the party we had just left behind.

"The novices were not a little discouraged at these frequent inroads of the enemy, although it is very seldom that any lives are lost in encounters with them."[22]

In the fall of 1844 Albert Speyer, a Santa Fe trader, camped here with perhaps 200 mules as a blizzard rose around them. The cold became so intense that the mules huddled together for warmth and still began to freeze. As the dead mules fell, the survivors would begin eating their ears to alleviate their starvation. When the storm ended they were only a pile of bodies, soon transformed by wolves into a heap of bones. It became a landmark on the Trail and subsequent parties passed the time in camp by arranging the bones into various designs.

To us, the area seemed especially desolate. After the green banks and cultivated fields of the north bank, the south seemed sandy and dry. Irrigation provided by giant walking sprinklers added to the forced appearance which all agriculture seemed to have in this wild and lonely place. To watch a farmer plow the dry, sifted sand was to watch the contribution of top soil to another Oklahoma cloud.

We spent the declining hours of the afternoon searching for signs of the Trail, which showed enough continuity to lead us up and onto the plains. We rode up and down the river and finally ran into two field workers in a pickup.

"Do you know where the old Santa Fe Trail crosses around here?" I asked.

"*No hablamos inglés. Estamos de Lordsburg Nueva Mexico.*"

"*Saben Vds. donde pasa el camino viejo para Santa Fé?*" I repeated. They talk to each other and one tells me. "*Está un camino viejo por allá.*"

"*Sí pero este camino tiene cien años y mas, lo conocen?*"

"*No sé.*"

I guess they don't teach American history in old Mexico! By now it's getting late and if we try to head out cross country without finding the ruts, we can really blow it, so we decide to stop for the night and try to find someone in the morning who can give us more precise directions. This could turn out to be a major problem. So we tie the horses, gather some bits of the meager firewood available and call it a day. We would like to get some water but can't figure out where the spigot on the sprinkler is located and so have to content ourselves with a shower instead. Off to the south we see a little encampment of lights surrounded by trees like some desert oasis in Arabia. Could that be Keyes (Oklahoma)? Once again the old debate over water, asking directions, drinking a cold beer. We don't know the town's size, and in this atmosphere we can't tell its distance from us so we try to ignore it as it sparkles in the night, tempting us with its promise of safety and luxury.

The next morning as we are saddling the horses, the rancher drives up, making his rounds with his foreman and checking the sprinklers. He gives us a looking-over reminiscent of unwelcomed Indians. We talk to him about our trip and ask him about the crossing at Willow Bar. He happens to have an aerial photograph in his truck which shows clearly the approach and crossing of the river. The Trail wandered up the present bottom for some ways and the sand bar is gone, but we can see where it comes out and heads towards those mountains. Could they be the Rabbit Ears? I suddenly have a vision of the Trail marked by a series of mountainous landmarks; sentinels, like old friends greeting the traveler at each successive leg of the trip. Sibley had described the view of the terrain and landmarks and even sketched their changing profile as he approached.

However, this was to prove mere nondescript mesa by some name such as "Eagle Rock" near Upper Springs, and not within sight of the great New Mexico landmarks, so that cherished theory evaporated.

Meanwhile, Jack had decided to load his chomped and gouty carcass onto his own horse and use YoYo (one of the Palomino's many nicknames) for the pack horse as had been our original plan. Jeanie had been flagging under the pack burden and YoYo was acting sufficiently domesticated to seem ready to risk the pack saddle. Our one reservation now was not bucking under the pack, but her habit of lying down and rolling over on her back with the saddle still on, trying to relieve some inconveniently protected itch in the middle of her back. So we packed her up and saddled Jeanie for the day's ride, but when Jack mounted Jeanie she began to buck and generally act riled. After watering at the sprinkler he tried again but with the same difficulty. By this time the rancher, Bob Pillow, and his foreman, Larry Nicodemos, had returned and we held a small council over the horses. Jack determined that Jeanie's withers had swollen under the pack and were now being rubbed by the low swell of his riding saddle. Bob thought that the horses, excepting Red, looked like they needed a rest for a day and offered us the use of his pasture and grain, as well as the bunk house for ourselves. I did not relish sitting around for a day, but Jack thought it was a marvelous idea and besides we could go into town and get some cold beer. So we tied the horses and climbed into Bob's truck for a trip to town and medicine for Jeanie. Riding back sprawled across the loaded pickup bed, sipping beer in the hot morning sun and streaking down the country roads at 70 mph was carefree contrast to our usual way of travel, and we looked forward to our first bath and food. There would be time for restful chores in camp. Jack was anxious to get off his bad leg for the day and was eager for a little social participation.

When Bob let us off back where we had left the horses, we loaded the baggage into the truck; he told us where to cross the river so as to avoid the quicksands. Because of the circuitous roads in the area, we would all get to the ranch at the same time even though it was only a mile or so away, and this was best, he said, because no one was welcomed on the ranch with just his wife there; anyway she wouldn't let us into the barn without his okay.

After taking care of the horses and giving Jeanie a shot of vitamins, we learned a little something about the ranch, which he ran for a corporation. He had been hired out of Colorado to manage it and put it on a sound financial basis after a period of apparent monetary loss. Bob was about our age, dressed in white straw hat, tailored western shirt and boots, good looking with a very "straight" appearance, and was obviously a shrewd businessman with an eye for financial calculation. He enjoyed the work outdoors and with animals, as well as working with the men under him and in all presented an attractive figure of personal and financial success in a business where such a combination of enjoyable work and money to reward it seems increasingly uncommon. It was good to see the contentment and interest of a man experiencing a feeling of success.

We ate lunch and then Bob announced that he and Larry had to move a large herd and wanted to know if we cared to ride along. Jack was dubious, but I was interested in seeing more of the working ranch. Our help must have been counter-productive because we were supposedly separating indistinguishable heifers and calves from some older branded cattle and driving them a couple of miles to the corrals, and I never even managed to identify the branded cattle. But it was a joy to watch the cutting once it began in the corrals, as man and horse in an almost mechanical team sought to isolate a single cow and run her out of the gate away from the herd. Bob, on his horse, would alternate with Larry on his. Larry was younger than Bob, smaller, blond, crew cut, face continually pink from the blazing sun; he was diffident and taciturn and deliberate in his actions but with a quiet humor sometimes exchanged for the seriousness, which suggested he rarely registered strong reactions.

Jack, dismounted now and with his leg in severe pain from the busman's holiday, was protecting a section of downed fence while I was posted at the corral's gate, trying to restrict passage of inappropriate cattle. The two men worked in friendly competition trying to execute the most efficient and elegant cutting movements. First one, then the other commenting on each other's actions. At one point each moved into the herd and brought out a running, dodging heifer which they relentlessly pushed towards the gate; and each laughed in amused surprise at their simultaneous score as the cattle spurted one to either side, and out the gate. Then Larry encountered an especially contrary cow which he was unable to control. And when it got out of the corral, he was unable to bring it back, though he tried time and again. At last he exploded in rage and throwing his rope around her head, he raced back to the corral dragging the uncompromising beast who seemed bigger than he and his horse together. Warning me out of the way, he jumped from his horse and ran up to her and began kicking her nose with the heel of his boot as he swore and cursed her. When he was finished, I looked at him there, fuming and a deeper red than usual, and said, "That's what the Mexicans would call 'estomping the chit' out of him." But it was to be another half an hour before he would smile.

That evening we sat around the bunkhouse porch beneath the

cottonwoods, sipping whiskey and talking about ranch life, business, horses, the merits and disadvantages of different kinds of bridles, and other topics until finally the light gave way to the night of star-studded Oklahoma skies. We were joined by the Spanish-speaking Mexican laborers who were returning from the fields long after dark, complaining of the portable radio which "couldn't speak Spanish" because its limited range wouldn't reach the powerful 50,000-watt stations of their native Chihuahua. By then, we were quite drunk and the conversation was a blur of philosophy, country music and groping Spanish and English in the mouths of amateurs.

At breakfast the next morning Jack's midnight encounter with the rat, which had awakened him by chewing on his sock, was overshadowed by his encounter with his morning coffee. Bob had fixed breakfast and we three, along with Larry, were sitting around the kitchen table finishing when I noticed Jack discretely pursing his lips and softly munching on something in his coffee. Ever the polite guest, he maintained a pathetically helpless look on his face as he looked about for a place to slyly deposit the contents of his mouth. After secretly using his napkin he took another draught of coffee. But his actions had not escaped unnoticed and as we turned to see what he was doing, he blatantly leaned over his plate and spit out two more—flies!! It seems Bob had grabbed some long unused cups for the extra guests, at least one unwashed. It was all we could do to maintain our male decor and keep from dissolving into hysterical laughter as he pondered those earlier gulps which he had swallowed without caution. With occasional bursts of mirth, we watched his hearty appetite wither and his face assume a bleak expression. It was one of those situations out of childhood, when menacing authority kept us from laughing and we got stomach cramps and tears were ready to stream down from our eyes. Now I was rapidly wiping them away so I could see and it was some time before I could look at Bob without setting off the violent bubbling laughter inside of me.

Today we wanted to get a good start so after things settled down again we drifted out to the barn to check on the horses. In spite of the medication Jeanie's back was worse. Bob said it looked like she might have a cancer and that this was some kind of old problem of hers which had been reactivated. She looked wasted and we decided to leave her and travel with just what we could carry on our saddles. This meant really paring down our load to a few days food and minimal sleeping and cooking gear. No tent, change of clothes, extra camera, or books. Now we were down to about 20 lbs. apiece loaded into our saddle bags and small packs behind the saddle: three days' food, exactly what we figure it would take us to go the 50 miles and reach the car at McNees Crossing, New Mexico. Jack decided to leave the small saddle he had been using and buy a larger roping saddle from Larry which would be more comfortable. We stored the pack saddle and the rest of our equipment in the bunkhouse, up out of reach of the rats, and tried to balance the packs on the horses so they wouldn't shift too much. We gave them a final graining and left Jeanie retired to pasture after little more than a week's service. (That turned out to be a sorry investment!!) Then we headed for the crossing where we had come across the previous day.

Bob had warned us about the quicksands in this area, pointing out an especially bad hole where, he said, rested a wagon, a car, and a locomotive. I wasn't much worried about the quicksands because I could usually read the river well enough if I looked closely and could find firm ground for crossing.

As we headed across the bar, I didn't pay much attention except to notice that there was more water coming down than yesterday. Red and I climbed down the steep bank and headed out onto the bar. He was hesitant and I had to urge him on. As we crossed, the dry surface turned to pudding—it slapped and shook under his steps. Suddenly he broke through the sand; and as water bubbled up around us, he started to sink. I was completely taken by surprise but realized we were both going to disappear from sight if the load wasn't lightened on his back.

When in quicksand, you're supposed to roll over backwards and go off the horse at the rear because the horse reacts with instinctive fear and is wildly seeking solid footing. From his point of view the only solid footing around is you! Many a man has drowned while the horse was saved by standing on his back. All this was running through my mind in the few seconds we were plunging into the hole, but with the pack tied on behind and my less-than-gymnastic capabilities, there was no way I was going to flip over Red's twisting, thrashing rump. So I decided to risk a side exit, jumping clear of him as far as possible. I swung to the side and arched my back to spring free, but as I reached his side he prepared for me.

What followed is one of life's vivid recollections: an act of primordial communication between man and beast. Both of us were gripped by the terror of being swallowed alive and seemed to sense the other's willingness to escape at his expense if necessary. Without looking at him I could see Red's movements in my mind's eye as if by intuitive sensing. As I swung past his side he prepared himself and when my weight reached his flank, he groped for my body. I could feel hooves flying towards me as though all four feet were reaching out trying to clutch me and step on me in order to raise himself from the mire. And I could see one of his eyes rolled back in his head looking directly at me, not with supplication but with the sense of desperate concentration one gains from naked survival. I jumped clear and the lightened weight allowed him to half float, half kick to the surface and he struggled back to the shore.

I was really shaken at that point, but Jack thought it was hilarious and said he wished he'd had his camera out because it would have been the action photo of the year. I declined to repeat the maneuver, however, although Red wasn't so sure when I went to lead him across again. His resistance indicated less than complete confidence in my abilities at that point, particularly on one blind detour which lead into more pudding. Ultimately, his loyalty and obedience to man triumphed and we floated him across without drowning him. He was one happy pony when we climbed up onto the soft, white, dry sands of the Cimarron's southern bank, and our sense of relief was not trailing far behind. Ahead of us lay the high plains of the Oklahoma No-Man's Land; dry, rolling and starkly beautiful, it was the most primeval stretch of our whole route.

Riding southwest up and across the hills and mesas, we could look back and see the tops of the trees lining the river valley which now angled away from us to the west, toward its origins in the Raton Mountains. We would be within sight of it for about two more days, but it would lie increasingly to the north and so we would be dependent upon the ruts to guide us. We were riding for Upper Springs and the road seemed to lead towards a hill which we could use as a landmark. The way was open with few fences on the Trail. It was Saturday and our goal was to make the highway near Upper Springs so we could catch a ride into Boise City and visit Mrs. Young, the newspaper publisher there whom I'd met the previous spring. There we'd try to get some grain for the horses, for we'd decided that the only way they could make the long days' rides ahead was with the extra energy from oats. We had some 18 miles to go and anticipated no problems although we'd been warned to watch out for the "James boys," whose ranch we were to cross near the highway.

As we rode up the undulating slope, the ruts clearly pointing the way ahead, we could feel a kinship to the past. It must have seemed much the same to the Sibley Brown party 140 years ago. Sibley described their departure from the river at a point further upstream than Willow Bar:

"Friday, 7th October
"A fair Morning tho' raw. Started at 45 minutes past 8. Traveled up the Valley South 81 West 6 miles to a Small Grove of Green Cotton Trees, near some high Rocky Bluffs. Here the Semerone looks something like a Mountain Stream—its water cold and clear, bed gravely, current brisk. As far as I could see up it from a high Hill, it is bounded on the north by lofty, Mountainous rocky Bluffs and precipices, having here and there some scattering clumps of Trees. It flows from the NorthWest. This is the point where we leave the Stream. We directed our March to the left, ascending the high land, upon a course south 51 west towards a clump of Green Trees which are in view and which we reached after a laborious journey of 5 Miles, over a rather Hilly route. Here we found, Situated amidst huge rocky cliffs, the Upper Semerone Spring affording abundance of excellent Water, and the long, narrow Valley that it waters supplied us with plenty of Wood for fuel and pretty good pasturage for our Horses. This is a noted camping place, and is the point from whence we are to take our departure across a sort of Sandy desert [sic] to another Creek to the West (the Canadian). We had Scarcely time to arrange our Camp before a cold rain commenced—distance today, 11 miles."[23]

Our day was only a little more eventful. There were high thin clouds shading the earth as we followed the long sweep of sculpted tracks across the roll of the hills down into broad sloping draws and past small rock outcroppings. On the ground was little vegetation other than sparse grass and occasional yucca. Off to the north we could see that the river passed at an altitude somewhat lower than ours. Late in the morning we rounded a large outcropping where the Trail began to dip down into a small valley. Being ready to give the horses a break and thinking it would have been an obvious place for a camp for voyageurs, we decided to look around. The site consisted of a small rock cliff overlooking the valley to the west, possibly Dakota sandstone, which tapered off into small caves and scattered boulders on the north face. Tying the horses and watching for snakes, we headed up the small, rocky draw overlooking the Trail.

From the top we could see that it was an ideal camp, being a flat, grassy mesa of some height, affording a broad view of the country around, and merging smoothly on the east with the hilltop we had just crossed. On walking across the crest I could see wagon tracks leaving the Trail and bending southeast to the access slope on my right. Towards the western edge was a pile of rocks looking like a grave and the flat sandstone by the cliff was inscribed with various names, two of the most clear being "Davies" and "Harper, 1858." Later we passed a stage station and an old stone homestead near a slimy green spring. We finally came to a fence across the Trail with the tightest wire yet found, really difficult to step down. There had been a gate at the Trail, but it had been wired shut. This seemed a likely place for the James' spread. It was the most obvious invitation to "keep out" that we had crossed so far. Continuing on we saw the mountain towards which we had been riding all day and then, far off towards the rocky slopes of some hills, Highway 287 coming down from Springfield, Colorado. It was where we'd catch our ride.

That night we camped on an open slope near Upper Springs. The sky was overcast and threatened rain, a particularly uncomfortable circumstance as we had hitched into Boise City that afternoon and gotten a brief taste of creature comforts. It made the night seem a little colder and our conditions a little more threatening. We had caught a ride with a trucker who had lived in the area and was interested in our ride, as well as in the landmarks we had passed. He even knew Bob Pillow of Willow Bar. Letting us off in Saturday afternoon Boise, he sent us to the Friendly Tavern where our venture rated free beer and a little conversation. With the help of the Youngs we obtained a two day supply of grain for the horses and a ride out to camp where they took some pictures for the newspaper. Discussing some of the people and events of the previous few days, I find that they too knew people and happenings along our way. How could they, I thought, be so familiar with things so distant, as if these were in their own backyard and not the tremendous laborious distance we had experienced? Then, I realized again that it was our mode of transportation from the past, not the motorized and electronic present which made the distance so great to us. And I felt a strange disorientation as though I were being lifted out of a familiar perspective into an unnatural and foreign dislocation. I was like some African villager suddenly placed in a European city and undergoing a dismaying culture shock. It was all very unreal. Now lying under an overcast sky with the wind blowing cinders from the fire and occasional smatterings of rain reminding us of just how miserable the elements could make us if they took a notion, I felt a

THE BOISE CITY NEWS
FORMERLY THE CIMARRON NEWS

Boise City, Cimarron County, Oklahoma 73933 Thursday, July 13, 1972

Pair Rides Down Trail to Santa Fe

Two men, trying for a feel of the "old West," are riding horseback down the Cimarron Cutoff of the Santa Fe Trail. They came through Cimarron County last week end. The pair are Curtiss Frank, a sociology professor at Colorado State University, Fort Collins, and Jack Underhill, a Santa Fe, N. M., journalist.

The horseback riders, complaining of "gout" (but not explicit in describing the location of the ailment) began their trek July 8, north of Ulysses, Kans. They were forced to leave their pack horse in Keyes, after his withers began swelling. They also left many of their supplies, which will make a hardship on them for the remainder of the trip. They had already determined that great delicacy, rattlesnake meat, would not be on their menu for a second time.

Heat during the early afternoon hours is usually reason to rein up and rest the horses for about three hours. Shortly after the start of their trip they had several days of rainy weather, which slowed them down. They hoped to be able to average 20 miles a day from here on.

Nearly all they meet ask the bewhiskered riders their reasons for making the trip. Underhill said he made a similar excursion through Spain a few years ago and everyone he met was convinced he was making a religious pilgrimage. In this country the first thought is "somehow, they're doing it for money".

The men have been good friends since their college days. Both are history buffs and have read everything they could get their hands on concerning the Santa Fe Trail. In the diaries kept by early-day travelers, such as Susan Magoffin, Col. Henry Inman and Josiah Gregg, they emphasized the hardships, but with a "chin up, carry on" sort of attitude. They told of dangers from Indians and thirst, but didn't express the feelings they had on seeing a new landmark in the distance, antelope and other wild game on the trail, nor the boredom of the slow travel. Frank and Underhill are attempting to capture those feelings on this trip. They are greatly pleased and surprised to find the old ruts are so easy to follow, after more than a hundred years of non-use.

The original Santa Fe Trail ran in a fairly direct line southwest from Independence, Mo., to Council Grove and Kinsley, Kans., straight west to Garden City, on to La Junta, Colo., then southwest again to Trinidad. From there it wound through the mountains in a southerly direction to Watrous, N. M., and Santa Fe. (Present-day towns are mentioned for the sake of clarity, but it should be understood there were no towns at that time.)

From the original trail the more direct Cimarron Cut-off departed at Cimarron, Kans., (about 30 miles north of Meade) on the Arkansas River to the western boundary of Kansas, across the southeast corner of Colorado, through Cimarron County, through northeast New Mexico to Wagon Mound. From there the Cut-off parallels U. S. Highway 56 to an intersection with the original trail near Watrous. From that point the Cut-off follows the original trail to Santa Fe.

In 1825 Congress appropriated funds for a survey of a more direct route to be made. This was done by Joseph C. Brown in 1826 and 1827.

JACK UNDERHILL (left) and Curtiss Frank are "on the trail" enroute to Santa Fe. The two men, history buffs of long-standing, are attempting to get the feel of the pioneer life by riding horseback the length of the Cimarron Cutoff of the original Santa Fe Trail.

Gregg made the first of six trips over the trail during the summer of 1831. On this trip his caravan camped at Flag Springs (then called "Upper Semaron Springs") on June 30. A few days later, on July 4, they camped at McNees Creek (the Carrumpa). This was the first Fourth of July celebration ever held in territory southwest of the Arkansas River.

The number of caravans cannot be estimated that passed over the trail from the time Brown made his survey until 1880, when the Santa Fe railroad built to Lamy, N. M., near Santa Fe. After that time the trail was no longer needed to move supplies into the area.

There are no more caravans over the trail, but the legend is kept alive by those who are fascinated by the story, and an occasional horseback rider, Jeep driver or ambitious hiker who travels part of the trail to get "the feel" of things.

disquieting insecurity, like some startling surprise was going to emerge out of the jet darkness around us. The horses were picketed across a fence along the Santa Fe tracks where the grass was better. I began to envision a train coming in the night and killing one of them. The distant sound of traffic on the highway reminded me of some human menace. For some reason I always found the nighttime traffic on a road to be disturbing while camped out in an otherwise uninhabited place. It was as though cars disturbed the tranquility of nature and distorted its balance of danger and tranquility. On that night I was becoming downright superstitious about it. But soon all these unreasoned fears were swept away by sleep, occasionally replaced by more tangible alarms as light rain would waken us and we would have to cover our heads with a poncho and lie beneath the tapping sound of drops, counting them; are they coming more now? Or do they slacken, remaining just a summer shower? Drowsy once again, I wearied of such thoughts and gave myself up to whatever fate the night portended. And so to sleep once more.

  Sunday morning Jack was ready for surgery. His gout had him in throbbing pain and the horse bite had festered under the skin into a purple and black ferment. His leg and foot had swollen until it was questionable whether he was going to get his boot on, and he acted like it would take a stepladder to get up into the saddle. He had, of course, left his medicine in his pack at Willow Bar, apparently not having anticipated any need for it. I gave him some codeine to take the edge off the pain, warning him not to take more than he needed be cause when he finally came down from it, he would be really depressed. That turned out to be pure fancy for his pain was such that he never even went up. We decided to switch horses as Red's gait was smoother and more comfortable. I hadn't been on Linda since the first day when I had decided that her capricious nature was too much risk for my back. But I had been having no problems, and she had settled down somewhat in the meantime. When I mounted she reached back with her head and took a nip from the cuff off my pants. This was too much to endure for a whole day, and besides, I had Jack's example before me. I got along with her somewhat better than he did and she never performed her little gestures with quite the malice she seemed to reserve for him; but even a small bite can be a painful shock so the next time she went for my leg I brought my foot up smartly and kicked her as hard as I could in the mouth. She was caught by surprise and jumped straight up into the air with a toss of the head like she was trying to shake out loose teeth. After that we had a sort of a wary understanding, or really more of a stalemate. She would not actually bite but would look around at my knee menacingly. And I did not have to kick her again but would have to look out of the corner of my eye at her to let her know I was still keeping an eye out. In this way we proceeded, affording Jack his only comic relief of the day.

Upper spring is located in a small, rocky ravine and boasts small pools at which cattle shade themselves beneath the overhanging trees. Riding through the small passes which restricted both our access and view in the steadily ascending terrain, we could almost miss it but for the wagon ruts which twisted down into the sloping canyon. The Spring was crucial to the old travelers because it provided one of the watering places on the Trail, now several miles from the Dry Cimarron. There is reported to be gold near the Springs, buried during an Indian attack, and never recovered. Sibley camped here for two nights in early October, 1825, and encountered rain, hail, and high winds. In anticipation of the difficult struggle across the "sparse range" to the Canadian (or Red River, as it was confusedly known in those days) his party lightened the wagons by packing their riding horses and proceeding on foot. They hiked southwest a mile and a half:

Upper Springs, Oklahoma, 1935 *(Denver Public Library)*

"... over rocky and rather hilly ground, and ascended to the top of a high ridge, at a pretty abrupt point. From this spot we have a very good view of a great extent of country. Two very conspicuous Mounds called the 'Rabbit Ears' (from their *supposed* resemblance to the ears of a rabbit) bear S. 60 W. and are supposed to be about 40 miles off. Another larger Mountain (Mt. Dora) bears S. 80 W. This is at present covered with Snow & looks to me more like a White cloud than a Mountain. Still farther West is seen, tho' much nearer to us, a very lofty and extensive flat; & the Valley of the Semerone is distinctly traced for a great distance, being bounded on the North by a high chain of rugged, rocky Hills. Although the scenery here is extremely beautiful.

"The 'Rabbit Ears' is the first great landmark; and to it, we now shape our course. At first we followed one of our guides directly forward several miles over a succession of heavy sand hills, but finding this too laborious, and seeing no hopes of soon getting thro' these hills, and no prospect of water, I turned off from the course and went down to the right into a valley."[24]

The impressive nature of the place is reflected in Gregg's first view back in 1831:

"The wildness of this place with its towering cliffs, craggy spurs and deep-cut crevices became doubly impressive to us, as we reflected that we were in the very midst of the most savage haunts. Often will the lonely traveler, as he plods his weary way in silence, imagine in each click of a pebble, the snap of a firelock, and in every rebound of a twig, the whisk of an arrow."[25]

Indeed, one of the most agonizing stories of Indian encounter is associated with the Spring and the country through which we had just passed. In 1828 a party of 25 men, including the narrator, a Mr. Bryant of Kansas, was returning from a trade expedition to Santa Fe:

"On the first day of September, those of us who had remained in Santa Fe commenced our homeward journey. We started with one hundred and fifty mules and horses, four wagons, and a large amount of silver coin. Nothing of an eventful character occurred until we arrived at the Upper Cimarron Springs, where we intended to encamp for the night. But our anticipations of peaceable repose were rudely dispelled; for when we rode up on the summit of the hill, the sight that met our eyes was appalling enough to excite the gravest apprehensions. It was a large camp of Comanches, evidently there for the purpose of robbery and murder. We could neither turn back nor go on either side of them on account of the mountainous character of the country, and we realized, when too late, that we were in a trap.

"There was only one road open to us; that right through the camp. Assuming the bravest look possible, and keeping our rifles in position for immediate action, we started on the perilous venture. The chief met us with a smile of welcome, and said, in Spanish: "You must stay with us tonight. Our young men will guard your stock, and we have plenty of buffalo meat."

"Realizing the danger of our situation, we took advantage of every moment of time to hurry through their camp. Captain Means, Ellison, and myself were a little distance behind the wagons, on horseback; observing that the balance of our men were evading them, the blood thirsty savages at once threw off their masks of dissimulation and in an instant we knew the time for a struggle had arrived.

"The Indians, as we rode on, seized our bridle-reins and began to fire upon us. Ellison and I put spurs to our horses and got away, but Captain Means, a brave man, was ruthlessly shot and cruelly scalped while the life blood was pouring from his ghastly wounds.

"We succeeded in fighting them off until we had left their camp half a mile behind, and as darkness had settled down on us, we decided to go into camp ourselves. We tied our gray bell-mare to a stake, and went out and jingled the bell, whenever any of us could do so, thus keeping the animals from stampeding. We corralled our wagons for better protection, and the Indians kept us busy all night resisting their furious charges. We all knew that death at our posts would be infinitely preferable to falling into their hands; so we resolved to sell our lives as dearly as possible.

"The next day we made but five miles; it was a continuous fight, and a very difficult matter to prevent their capturing us. This annoyance was kept up for four days; they would surround us then let up as if taking time to renew their strength, to suddenly charge upon us again, and they continued thus to harass us until we were almost exhausted from loss of sleep.

"After leaving the Cimarron, entering the Jornada, possibly west of Lower Springs, we once more emerged on the open plains and flattered ourselves we were well rid of the savages; but about twelve o'clock they came down on us again, uttering their demoniacal yells, which frightened our horses and mules so terribly, that we lost every hoof. A member of our party, named Hitt, in endeavoring to recapture some of the stolen stock, was taken by the savages, but luckily escaped from their clutches, after having been wounded in sixteen parts of his body; he was shot, tomahawked, and speared. When the painted demons saw that one of their number had been killed by us, they left the field for a time, while we, taking advantage of the temporary lull, went back to our wagons and built breastworks of them, the harness, and saddles. From noon until two hours in the night, when the moon went down, the savages were apparently confident we would soon fall a prey to them, and they made charge after charge upon our rude fortifications.

"Darkness was now upon us. There were two alternatives before us: should we resolve to die where we were, or attempt to escape in the black hours of the night? It was a desperate situation. Our little band looked the matter squarely in the face, and, after a council of war had been held, we determined to escape, if possible.

"In order to carry out our resolve, it was necessary to abandon the wagons, together with a large amount of silver coin, as it would be impossible to take all of the precious stuff with us in our flight; so we packed up as much of it as we could carry and, bidding our hard-earned wealth a reluctant farewell, stepped out in the darkness like spectres and hurried away from the scene of death.

"Our proper course was easterly, but we went in a northerly direction in order to avoid the Indians. We traveled all that night, the next day, and a portion of its night until we reached the Arkansas River, and, having eaten nothing during that whole time excepting a few prickly-pears, were beginning to feel weak from the weight of our burdens and exhaustion. At this point we decided to lighten our loads by burying all of the money we had carried thus far, keeping only a small sum for each man. Proceeding to a small island in the river, our treasure, amounting to over ten thousand silver dollars, was cached in the ground between two cottonwood trees.

"Believing now that we were out of the usual range of the predatory Indians, we shot a buffalo and an antelope which we cooked and ate without salt or bread; but no meal has ever tasted better to me than that one.

"We continued our journey northward for three or four days more, when, reaching Pawnee Fork, we traveled down it for more than a week, arriving again on the Old Santa Fe Trail. Following the Trail three days, we arrived at Walnut Creek, then left the river again and went eastwardly to Cow Creek. When we reached that point, we had become so completely exhausted and worn out from subsisting on buffalo meat alone, that it seemed as if there was nothing left for us to do but lie down and die Finally it was determined to send five of the best preserved men on ahead to Independence, two hundred miles, for the purpose of procuring assistance; the other fifteen to get along as well as they could until succour reached them.

"I was one of the five selected to go on in advance, and I shall never forget the terrible suffering we endured. We had no blankets, and it was getting late in the fall. Some of us were entirely barefooted, and our feet so sore that we left stains of blood at every step. Deafness, too, seized upon us so intensely, occasioned by our weak condition, that we could not hear the report of a gun fired at a distance of only a few feet.

"At one place two of our men laid down their arms, declaring they could carry them no farther, and would die if they did not get water. We left them and went in search of some. After following a dry branch several miles, we found a muddy puddle from which we succeeded in getting half a bucket full, and, although black and thick, it was life for us and we guarded it with jealous eyes. We returned to our comrades about day light, and the water so refreshed them they were able to resume the weary march. We traveled on until we arrived at the Big Blue River, in Missouri, on the bank of which we discovered a cabin about fifteen miles from Independence. The occupants of the rude shanty were women, seemingly very poor, but they freely offered us a pot of pumpkin they were stewing. When they first saw us, they were terribly frightened, because we looked more like skeletons than living beings. They jumped on the bed while we were greedily devouring the pumpkin, but we had to refuse some salt meat which they had also proffered, as our teeth were too sore to eat it. In a short time two men came to the cabin and took three of our men home with them. We had subsisted for eleven days on one turkey, a coon, a crow, and some elm bark, with an occasional bunch of wild grapes, and the pictures we presented to these good people they will never, probably, forget; we had not tasted bread or salt for thirty-two days.

"The next day our newly found friends secured horses and guided us to Independence, all riding without saddles. One of the party had gone on to notify the citizens of our safety, and when we arrived general muster was going on, the town was crowded, and when the people looked upon us the most intense excitement prevailed. All business was suspended; the entire population flocked around us to hear the remarkable story of our adventures, and to render us the assistance we so much needed. We were half-naked, foot-sore, and haggard, presenting such a pitiable picture that the greatest sympathy was immediately aroused in our behalf.

"We then said that behind us on the Trail somewhere, fifteen comrades were struggling toward Independence, or were already dead from their sufferings. In a very few minutes seven men with fifteen horses started out to rescue them.

"They were gone from Independence several days, but had the good fortune to find all the men just in time to save them from starvation and exhaustion. Two were discovered a hundred miles from Independence, and the remainder scattered along the Trail fifty miles further in their rear. Not more than two of the unfortunate party were together."[26]

Inman quotes Mr. Hitt's description of his part of the adventure, his escape after being overtaken by the Indians while hunting the lost stock:

"It was late in the afternoon when I, having left my companions to continue the search and returning to camp alone, had gotten within a mile of it, that I thought I saw a horse feeding upon an adjoining hill. I at once turned my steps in that direction, and had proceeded but a short distance when three Indians jumped from their ambush in the grass between me and the wagons and ran after me. The men in camp had been watching my every movement, and as soon as they saw the savages were chasing me, they started in pursuit, running at their greatest speed to my rescue.

"The savages soon overtook me, and the first one that came up tackled me, but in an instant found himself flat on the ground. Before he could get up, the second one shared the same fate. By this time the third one arrived, and the two I had thrown grabbed me by the legs so that I could no longer handle myself, while the third one had a comparatively easy task in pushing me over. Fortunately, my head fell toward the camp and my fast-approaching comrades. The two Indians held my legs to prevent my rising, while the third one, who was standing over me, drew from his belt a tomahawk, and shrugging his head in his blanket, at the same time looking over his shoulder at my friends, with a tremendous effort and that peculiar grunt of all savages, plunged his hatchet, as he supposed, into my head, but instead of scuffling to free myself and rise to my feet, I merely turned my head to one side and the wicked weapon was buried in the ground, just grazing my ear.

"The Indian, seeing that he had missed, raised his hatchet and once more shrugging his head in his blanket, and turning to look over his other shoulder, attempted to strike again, but the blow was evaded by a sudden toss of his intended victim's head. Not satisfied with two abortive trials, the third attempt must be made to brain me, and repeating the same motions, with a great 'Ugh,' he seemed to put all his strength into the blow, which, like the others, missed, and spent its force in the earth. By this time the rescuing party had come near enough to prevent the savage from risking another effort, and then he addressed the other Indians in Spanish, which I understood, saying, 'We must run or the Americans will kill us!' and loosening his grasp, he scampered off with his companions as fast as his legs could take him, hurried on by several pieces of lead fired from the old flintlocks of the traders."

All this activity had occurred over just about the whole area we had traveled so far. The bullion they buried was recovered the following spring at Chateau's island by the party accompanied by Major Riley, which I mentioned previously in connection with the Jornada.

The waters of Upper Cimarron Spring were too muddied to drink, so we decided to wait until we found a windmill to fill our canteens. Following the rocky hillside trail, Jack rode ahead to shoot some pictures. As we came to the top of the broken hills, the country opened into a huge rolling basin which had all the sparse, stark feeling of a mountain tundra. All at once it began to seem as though we were in another world, a scene from Dante with strange, alien vegetation and foreign geography, the kind of profoundly different terrain which takes some small unusual feature of our own landscape and expands it into a continent. This seemingly alpine dale rose steadily on one side until it culminated in a ridge which gave me the impression that had I ridden to the brow of the hill and looked over to the other side, I should have seen something vast, unearthly and profound like a vision of purgatory or, perhaps, Hades itself. To the right, the upland basin sloped off in waves and canyons toward where the tops of the trees traced the jagged line of the Dry Cimarron—a reminder, only a hint, of more sheltered terrain appearing by contrast to this haunted landscape. Jack found that his pack had loosened and his sleeping bag had fallen from the saddle. While he rode back to look for it, I decided to ride toward a cluster of buildings which were huddled on the side of the ridge above us. Perhaps it was a ranch and there would be water. I spurred my horse into a gallop and headed up the elevated plain.

As I approached I could see that what I had taken to be buildings were only low hovels grouped near a windmill-like dwarf shelter. Tracks around the tank indicated that this was sheep range; these buildings probably sheltered the sheep during the abrupt and violent storms. The water was cold and good, and as I stooped and drank I poured draughts over my neck and hair with my hat. The horse crowded in beside me to drink and we stood together, ankle deep in the thick, black mud surrounding the mill. From this height we could look down upon the whole of the valley and I had the feeling that had the ground been slick we could have slid down the side in an endless, uninterrupted fall to some remote base level beyond our vision. Below me, a mile away, I could see the lone figure of Jack on horseback returning across the small divide, careless and seemingly innocent of the portent of this ground. I watched for a while as he opened the gate and remounted, looking for his next destination. Then I climbed into the saddle and galloped down to meet him and resume the journey.

All that day and the next we rode through this strange and beautiful country. By now, Jack's leg was so bad that I had to open all the gates because he could not dismount and mount, and I began to fear for the rest of the trip. Riding Linda was a different experience from riding Red. Over the last couple of weeks I had learned a lot about Red and was coming to really like and enjoy him for his personality. After a little light roughness I had gotten Red to give up all his unpredictable behavior which had kept me uneasy and probably contributed further to his threatening activities. Now the shoe was on the other foot and he displayed, if not wariness, at least the proper deference without his physical aggressiveness toward me. My own unpredictability and occasional physical aggressiveness towards him rendered him slightly defensive and a bit intimidated at times. He never knew if I would jump on him bareback and run him for two miles shouting and urging him beyond his own idea of appropriate speed. And he was unable to recognize that my exuberant appreciation of him, characterized by enthusiastic talking and hardy stroking, was not the first step in some diabolical wrestling match in which I was seeking to reduce him to abject contrition. It's a little hard for me to understand how a half ton of muscle with a neck like a bull and hooves like iron ingots can be intimidated by one hundred and sixty pounds of questionable tissue, barely able to lift my own weight. But I guess in the end it's mostly bluff.

Anyway, the arrangement was much more comfortable to me, and Red, being pure beast, had not become sullen or untrustworthy. He remained big-hearted and obedient, willing to go for as long as his master desired and under almost any conditions demanded of him. If properly managed, he could be urged into almost any task which his incredible strength would allow. At times he would go all day until his spirit and apparently his flesh was flagging, and I began to worry about working him further. Then, with the right psychological lift (usually the brief excitement of a parade before an enamored mare), he would draw upon reserves of strength I could not have imagined, and again he would trot, walk, and run for three or four more hours. Late one day, after dark and after hours of great exertion, we encountered a terrifying five-foot-wide moat of water; he coiled his body and sprang across the distance from a standing position which so caught me by surprise that I almost wound up swimming the distance he flew. His instinct for survival is such that, in sharing a limited food supply with other horses, he will crowd them out and grow fat while they wither and shrivel in the first stages of starvation. And in walking or trotting in company with other horses, he will work his way briskly but surreptitiously in front of the other horses until they are all arranged in a line. Then he will imperceptibly slow down until they are all moving at the slowest imaginable pace even as Red continues to exhibit the most graphic plodding motions rendering it apparent that further effort will cause him to collapse with exhaustion, and only constant, cognizant, and seemingly cruel goading from an ungrateful master can induce him to greater speed.

Yet such is the instinctive nature of his sloth that the rider need only direct him to the side of another horse, and he will briskly and energetically maintain the most rapid pace necessary to compete against his

Camping with Red and Linda

companion for hours on end. Such idiosyncrasies, while at times annoying, have mainly served to endear him to me as I have come to understand him. The enjoyment of his brutish nature has become such a pleasure to me that I have been fascinated and amazed by his physical powers in spite of the absence of human intelligence. I have come to understand what women mean when they are attracted to athletes for their "gorgeous bodies" and in spite of their other limitations. So it is that I have become enamored of Red.

The Palomino, on the other hand, was a different story. She exhibited a combination of youthful naivete and intelligence which was at times frustrating and at times charming. She proceeded with an attitude of fearfulness toward the unknown, wide-eyed openness toward the unexpected. The beast's intelligence was exasperating, as when she displayed stubborn willfulness, using an ever-increasing inventory of tricks. She was not easy to intimidate being aware that she could always resort to kicking, biting, and bucking if it came down to a test of strength. They often proved to be effective countermeasures if used in the right situation. On the other hand, her wits had some charms and her horrified reactions to anticipated occurrences evoked a certain amused sympathy in me. Her aggressive curiosity was sometimes a source of humor. Whenever it became apparent that we were approaching a gate she quickened her pace to a fast trot and rushing forward at a gait which seemed to indicate she was going to crash right through, she would suddenly stop with her head thrust over the other side, looking back and forth for some exciting new companion which she hoped to encounter on the other side. Rarely did a new friend materialize, but so constant was her curiosity and expectation that she continued this practice until Red began to imitate her with the apparent logic that there must be something to it if it happened so often.

Being ridden was something new in her life and just didn't match the charms of grazing in a pasture all day. Her response was to feel consistently overburdened, which she communicated by turning to snap at us like a cantankerous turtle whenever we rode her too long or with too much weight. Having to wear that sweaty and confining saddle which kept her from scratching the very spot where she always itched was another one of her grievances against us. Her solution to that one was to lie down when we weren't looking and commence rolling like a pig, complete with saddle, saddle bags, and pack tied behind the cantle. It became almost a ritual. Jack always put his camera in the saddle bag on the left side, and Linda always began a roll by going down on the left knee and then flopping over onto the soft dirt, hard clay, rocks, rattlesnakes, or whatever. With the saddle and other equipment, she never managed to get over on the other side, but that was sufficient because Jack always managed to stash the camera on that side. On the first occasion, the lens cover shattered. On subsequent ones various parts bent and broke until we were sure that the only pictures we were coming away with were to be various combinations of kinetic art attributable to the light leaks. For some reason it never occurred to us to put our camera into the other bag; and after each one of Linda's romps, I would ask Jack the ritualistic question, "Which side did you put the camera on, Jack?"

And his dejected answer would come back, "The left one."

Rare was the opportunity, but wholesome the satisfaction when we could catch her going down on that front knee while still within running distance from us. Then one of us could race over and give a swift application of the toe of our boot to the flank of her belly and we could "count coup." Eventually, she began to get the idea and when in sight of her and she began her descent, a sudden gesture on our part was enough

Linda takes a roll

Linda takes a roll

to send her scurrying to her feet with a look of pathetic frustration in her eyes.

She wasn't bad to ride, after the initial notion to buck had been quelled, except that her short size gave her rapid trot—a motion somewhat similar to that of a jackhammer—and her lope had a back and forth roll to it that reminded me of a hobbyhorse so that I had to look under her occasionally to convince myself that she didn't have a couple of barrel staves nailed between her front and back feet. Walking along, she presented an improbable sight. Head down, nose thrust forward, nostrils flared as though she were sniffing her way to an obscure destiny, she reminded me of a caricature out of Joe Back's book. These peculiarities did provide her with a colorful and alert look.

Sometime after noon we reached Cold Spring, which was the next major watering place on the Trail. By now we were hot and tired and as the cliffs around the stream are covered with inscriptions, we thought it was an ideal spot to rest the horses and explore. We ate one of those gourmet sandwiches of chicken salad with mayonnaise and drank milk with ovaltine until we were bloated. Then we sprawled in the sun, our heads in our saddles, and went to sleep. When I awoke, Jack was still asleep and I went over to one of the pools and took off my clothes to lie in the cold running water. Sliding off the smooth, gray rock and into the deep, sandy pocket below the rivulet of the stream was the most exquisite delight. As my body penetrated the surface of the pool, I was buoyed by the quality of the water and lightly pulled by the action of the current. The coolness drew off the summer swelter in my body and rinsed away the sweat and grime from the morning's ride.

I could feel the delicious refreshment as the cooled blood began to circulate away from my swollen and tired feet. I lay my head back in the water until my hair floated cold upon the surface and my scalp tingled with the incandescent contrast. I dropped my head forward as my hair flung an arc of splattering droplets across the surface. Lying in the warm sun I savored the sense of satisfaction and relief. Engaged as I was in higher pleasures, I did not notice Jack as he limped up with the excited news that the horses had been suddenly frightened and had run away.

We had tied them to some bushes near the stream where some mammoth hogs had been basking; and when these beasts had finally stirred it was as though the very rocks had come alive. The horses leaped

Revelling in Cold Springs

J.W. Kline, Lebanon, Pennsylvania 1866

in terror and bolted up the creek from where we came. This news was the proper nadir to offset my rare and recent joy, as I was the only one who could walk and would now have to hike after them. So, with binoculars and bridle, I set out to engage in the all-too-frequent drudgery.

Fortunately, they did not return to Willow Bar or even Upper Spring but had found a bunch of horses on top of a ridge a half mile off and were there quietly grazing and rubbing noses. In short order I had mounted Big Red and led the palomino back to camp. But in that heat, it was anything but pleasant. We spent the rest of the siesta examining inscriptions on the cliffs. These inscriptions were the most numerous of any we saw. Harper was present again, as well as Mexican nationals from the 1830s and U.S. troops from the 1840s.

Having spoken to the rancher on the way in, we stopped at the house to buy some bread. It was an elegant place for such a remote location; the house seemed quite comfortable and the people were charming. The barns and corrals were constructed of stone, giving them a European flavor, and horses danced back and forth with curiosity as we rode in. Inside, it was one of those Sunday afternoons of grandchildren, singing, and relaxation, altogether evoking feelings about family circle which had been totally removed from our adventures.

At one time, the Springs had been the intersection of several trails including branches of the Santa Fe. We took the route pointed out by the owner and rode up out of the canyon leaving the spring behind. The top once again put us onto the broad, rolling, vacant country over which we had been traveling previously. Great dark thunderheads were piling up high to our left and the darkened sky was beginning to turn the landscape into a rich, honeyed green. As we rode on we left all signs of human habitation behind except occasional fences and windmills. We saw no cattle, buildings, roads, or even airplanes. In that rugged rolling grassland, whose high plains were occasionally cut by shallow valleys or rocky ravines, with the billowing black clouds stacked into crescendo columns supporting a sky as textured and expansive as the earth below, and with rich and varied light revealing novel nooks and corners in the landscape across which spread before us the sculpted ruts of the road to Santa Fe, I truly felt that I was close to the primal nature of the land. I half expected to see a herd of buffalo appear before us, heads down, grazing, briefly looking up at these intruders from the future. A wind blew across the land and we headed on. The sounds of my harmonica were peaceful on the face of the prairie and held the proper softness and humility not to augment the small intrusion of us men.

To the south I could see the towering mist from a swelling, moist front which was rising out of the Gulf of Mexico, its ragged edges marking the transition in the climate. And on the breeze, which I took deep into my lungs, I could smell the salt air, as startling as the memory it brought to me of the far away Atlantic.

We rode and rode through the afternoon, hoping to reach a ranch where we could obtain grain for the horses. Jack was exhausted now and in such pain as to have no interest in special destinations. We approached a country highway and thinking I saw buildings which would shelter us from accumulating rain clouds, we rode on only to find they were culverts, too dangerous in time of flood to shelter us from storms. So we camped on the edge of an arroyo to get out of the wind and took our chances with the sky. I build a hasty fire to cook and we soon fell into bed in such exhaustion that I was unable to take any precautions against getting wet in the night. With packs exposed, saddles covered only by our heads and my small poncho on my sleeping bag, I lay down on the sweaty saddle blanket which was my mattress and simply prayed that it would not rain. It was one of the times when I thought of Stutzman's vague promise, "If I just had the time, I'd get some of the boys together and stage an Indian raid on you fellows."

"Jesus," I thought, "If anybody did that tonight . . . ?" And I speculated in trepidation what it was like in the old days when you felt like this, to have to go through a shock like that. And in my imagination it was already happening.

The following morning we went in search of a ranch where we could buy grain. The horses were faring much better with the energy boost received from it and it made a great deal of difference as to how much speed we could get from them. After a couple of hours we rode into a place which was a strange combination of decrepit board and batten shacks, and a modern trailer. Landscaped by a few struggling Chinese elms which barely seemed to hold their own, it was set on a sandy patch of earth which looked inimical to both man and vegetation. Woman and child scurried around behind the house as we approached and dismounted. We picked our way through the horses and dogs and knocked on the door of the house. We were greeted by a middle-aged man with a face as weather-beaten and character-ridden as the country. Slow moving and deliberate as he pursued his unannounced purposes, he was generous and kind beneath the typical masculine deference he displayed. As the coffee pot percolated its song of hospitality, we fed the horses a generous measure of Omalene, while Charles went about his silent task of evaluating our outfit. In the corral Linda commenced to scratching. Over she went on her side, stirrups flapping, saddle bags waving like an excited chicken on its back, feet up, kicking, she tried to complete a roll and almost made it over that time. Being perched up there on that saddlehorn must really do something for those hard to reach places.

"Which side is the camera on, Jack?"

You guessed it.

I had loosened my cinch before going in for coffee and now Red's saddle had slid over the side and under his belly complete with full pack and sleeping bags. It was so heavy that I couldn't slide it up again. Every time I would roll it up the side, the *chinchas* would tickle his belly and he would scoot to the side. Charles watched us for a moment and then came over and helped me resaddle. After I strained to help him disconnect it, he picked up the whole shootin' match and just swung it up onto the horse's back while I tied the *chinchas*. Then he disappeared into the barn, and we thought he had gone for good. We finished our preparations until ready to leave and went over to the barn to say goodbye. Out he came with a leather strap he had been cutting to space the two *chinchas*, which he proceeded to attach. I protested that I had never had any problems with it riling Red up, but he wasn't asking. Then he went over and made some adjustments in Jack's gear until he had apparently rendered everything to his satisfaction and we could proceed. Headed for the gate he pointed out for us, we departed to rediscover the Trail, leaving him, no doubt, bewildered as to how we had made it this far.

It was a beautiful day as we headed west towards the Rabbit Ears. It was the first wholly, sunny day we had had since we reached Willow Bar; the sky was a bright blue and thousands of white puffs of clouds dotted the ground with potato shadows. The atmosphere was clear and ahead we could see the country breaking up into rocky mesas and gulches. We were headed for Fort Nichols now, the rendezvous constructed by Kit Carson under orders to protect the wagon trains in the dreadful year of 1865.

Carson had been ordered to establish the camp as a halfway post between the Arkansas River and Fort Union. With 300 New Mexico and California volunteers he built the camp in May, 1865, at Cedar Bluff Springs, one of the major stopping points at the Trail. Wagons were to accumulate here until there were sufficient number to deserve a military escort. The first detachment of 70 wagons was escorted to Fort Larned on the Arkansas on June 19. In 1934 Albert Thompson reported an interview with a ninety-year-old woman living in Trinidad, Colorado, who was taken to live at the outpost as a young bride. She spoke of how Carson told her never to leave the walls of the fort because of Indian danger.

These are Mrs. Russell's remarks as they appeared in *Colorado Magazine* in 1934:

> "I was born in Illinois and was married at Fort Union, New Mexico, in February, 1865, to Lieut. R. D. Russell, a member of the regular army, though a Canadian by birth. My wedding journey, I might say, was made to Camp Nichols.
>
> "In May, 1865, orders were given Kit Carson to march eastward along the Santa Fe Trail, which passed Fort Union, and establish a cantonment for the protection of the wagon trains and stages along the route to the end of the railways in Missouri and Kansas. I did not go to

this new point of defense till about two weeks after the troops had been at work at Camp Nichols, as it was called, some 120 miles east of Fort Union. I was then 20 years of age.

"Kit Carson, who marched from Fort Union with his regulars and selected its site, would not let me make this journey in May, although I begged that I might accompany my husband and others, and scoffed at the idea of danger. But the colonel was obdurate. Perhaps fifteen days after their arrival at Cedar Bluffs, he ordered Lieutenant Russell to proceed with wagons and an escort to Fort Union, and on his return I accompanied him to Fort Nichols.

"On our arrival, in June, 1865, we lived in army tents until our houses were completed. The latter were built of stone, half in the ground and half above, and had dirt roofs supported by logs. Timber for roofs and other purposes was cut at the head of one of the canyons, eleven miles west, and laboriously hauled some twenty feet from the south wall.

"In these officers' quarters lived Maj. A. H. Pfeiffer, in command after Carson left, Capt. R. C. Kemp, Captain Strom (California company), Captain Hubbell, Capt. William Henderson and Lieuts. John Drenner, Campbell and Ortner. We had also ten Indian scouts and two squaws, and there were two laundresses, wives of Mexican soldiers of one of the companies, who washed for the infantry and cavalry, each soldier paying $1 a month for laundry work. Mrs. Henderson, wife of the officer, and I, with the above, were the only women in camp.

"The soldiers, some 300 in number, slept in tents and dugouts within the enclosure. The Cheyennes and Arapahoes were especially bad east along the trail, and every two weeks, as the wagon trains collected from the west at Nichols, an escort of our soldiers would accompany them to Fort Dodge or Fort Larned, and return with wagons westbound.

"Captain Strom from California was the first detailed to go east, and two weeks after my husband made the second trip to Fort Larned, on the Pawnee Fork, Kansas, where he joined Strom's company and together they made the return to Fort Nichols, thirty-two days being required for the journey. On this trip there were over 500 wagons, drawn by mules, horses and oxen, which stretched out great distances by day and corralled at night and, being heavily loaded, moved slowly. One of the caravans I recall was that of John and Andres Doll of Las Vegas, and another, Mr. Lunnings of Albuquerque.

"It was an imposing sight indeed to watch the arrival of this great cavalcade of covered wagons, with their massive, clanking wheels and high bodies, to listen to the cries of the men, the cracking of whips by the drivers of the 'bull' teams, to follow the majordomo as, on horseback, we went up and down the line urging forward the tired animals, flanking which rode members of our cavalry, and then to see about sunset this moving mass as it halted and prepared for the darkness, soon to come on.

"Life at Camp Nichols often was monotonous. Our mail was irregular, arriving from Fort Union by express, and this was supplemented from occasional passing caravans westbound. Our house consisted of two stone rooms, dirt floor and roof, with blankets for doors, and white cloth over the window frame in place of glass. Our water was brought from the stream, some 600 feet away, in buckets, and a soldier of our company was assigned us as cook.

"The fare consisted of hardtack, bacon, beans, beef, flour, with sugar and coffee. We had no rice, dried fruit nor potatoes or fresh vegetables; neither had we stoves, and all cooking was done in Dutch ovens, usually in the fireplaces. Some time in the summer of 1865, Sutler W. H. Moore of Fort Union sent over some 'delicacies' in the way of canned goods, and on their arrival my husband purchased $42 worth of these, most of which we consumed in two days. They consisted of peaches and other preserved fruit, No. 3 cans, oysters, and pickles in small bottles, and for these we paid $2 per can or jar, which, though costly, we reveled in after the daily fare of government rations.

"Beef was plentiful from our herd of cattle, driven from Fort Union and guarded day and night near the fort. The scouts killed deer frequently along the breaks north and east of us, and the squaws dressed the hides from these at the stream under the bank from the cantonment.

"The furniture was simple. Our bed was made from a log six feet long split in two and laid on the floor, then covered with boughs and blankets. A folding army table with no chairs completed the list.

"I distinctly recall Kit Carson, in actions, looks, and appearance. He was present only fifteen days at Camp Nichols after my arrival in June, 1865, and occupied an army tent just east of ours. He was exceedingly kind and courteous to me, a man short of stature, slow of speech and sparing in conversation, though ever solicitous of our comfort. He visited much with us, and I remember his crude English, 'whar' for where, and 'thar' for there. I do not recall that he superintended to any great extent the work of the soldiers, which seemed to go on with the regularity of clockwork.

"His tent was some fifty feet from ours, and generally had its sides rolled up. Within it Colonel Carson lay much of the time during the day on his rough bedstead, made of four short forked posts set in the ground with poles across, and scanned the neighboring elevations, looking for Indians which, however, never came.

"One night during a wind and rain storm his tent blew down, and he had to call the sergeant of the guards to come and get him out. The last time I saw him was as he, leading his horse, stopped at our tent, before our stone rooms were completed, the morning he set out for Fort Union to bid me goodby and again warn me not to go out 'thar,' pointing off to the Santa Fe Trail, as the Indians might get me.

"I was the last person he addressed before he mounted and rode away. I was never to see him again. He and all the officers at Camp Nichols wore their uniforms most of the time, though occasionally they donned cloth blouses when scouting. Captain Strom was the most proper officer at Nichols, and I never recall seeing him with his uniform coat unbuttoned.

"And so the summer of 1865 passed quickly enough for us at the new cantonment, finishing walls and houses and performing military duty. My time was spent in short walks, watching the squaws as they busied themselves in and about the fort, or tanned deer hides at the stream, and with occasional short rides on horseback with Major Pfeiffer, who taught me how to mount and sit in the saddle. His wife had, a short time before this, been killed by the Indians at Fort Craig and he was shot in the hip with an arrow, which ever afterwards caused lameness and a great hatred of 'Injuns.'

"One story I must tell of Major Pfeiffer. At Nichols one of the soldiers had a pet crow. The bird would fly into houses and rooms and help himself at will. One day we found that it had visited Pfeiffer's quarters, nearly destroyed a shirt and, worst of all, upset a bottle of whiskey, the contents of which were lost. In relating this the major said, 'That crow. He tore my shirt that cost $7. That don't matter, but he also steal my whiskey.'

"Each morning the ten Indian scouts would quietly ride away to return at sunset. Two pickets were kept out during the day, one two miles west, and the other about the same distance east, mounted always on fast horses, and at night sentinels were posted near the camp. No Indians, however, ever ventured to attack us, though a few miles down the trail they continued their raids. The howitzers at Camp Nichols were fired on one occasion only, and that was July 4, 1865. The camp flagpole stood some 100 feet south of the gate and the flag from this flew daily to the breeze. Regularly at 9 p.m. the bugler sounded 'tattoo' and at 9:15 'taps.'

"This routine life lasted until the latter part of September and then orders came to us one day, after a good deal of stone work had been performed, to return to Fort Union. Our infantry and cavalry one morning got into regular formation, wagons were loaded with what we wished to take, and slowly we rode westward, in a few days to again reach Fort Union. We left at Camp Nichols a stack of hay and another on the prairie, which the men had cut during the summer, and on the flagpole a notice warning everybody against destroying the property. Thus closed my life, though by no means my vivid recollection of it, at this short-lived fort on the old trail."[27]

Thompson reports that the walls were still intact when he first visited the site in the 1890s but that since then settlers have carried away the stones for building purposes. When we found it, almost by accident after vainly riding around off to the north for two hours, it was a low mound which nevertheless clearly outlined the structure. On a high, rugged mesa, a place of wild isolation, it seems today as it must have seemed then; and for a while I was transported back into history.

As I rode up to the ruins, I could sense its purpose and design without having ever seen any details. There were sentry posts carefully scattered on three sides, fewer as you reached the furthest point from the fort, more numerous and closer together as you approached the walls. The south side an open field, was the point of approach, while the east and western sides were a short distance from the steep cliffs. The rationale for these tiny rock posts seemed to be to prevent Indians from surprising the fort, or, if the fort were attacked, to produce increasingly concentrated fire as an enemy approached the stronghold. It was like a series of lines, each one increasingly defensible, for the troops to fall back to. I could sense that the entire strategy was to buy time and (in the days of single shot rifles which had to be reloaded with separate powder, patch and shot) to increase fire power. (Wagon trains always retained half of a volley when under attack or else they would be unarmed for a crucial period, for the Indians could get off arrows with the speed of a repeater.) It gave the troops time to prepare themselves and strengthen the defenses in steps, thus working against any advantage of surprise.

There was only one gate and the rest was stone walls: breastworks, officers' quarters, commissary and hospital. In the center is the stone pavement some twenty by one hundred feet where the horses were tied. I located the foundation which Mrs. Russell identified as her own quarters outside the fort, and the past returned to me vividly present. As I rode around the parade grounds, I could hear bugles. In the over whelming impact of history which I could sense in that place, I could feel for a moment what it was like to be a man in those times: the very small human scale in contrast to this big frontier land; how little there was of civilization, water, shelter and comforts available to diminish the daily effects of

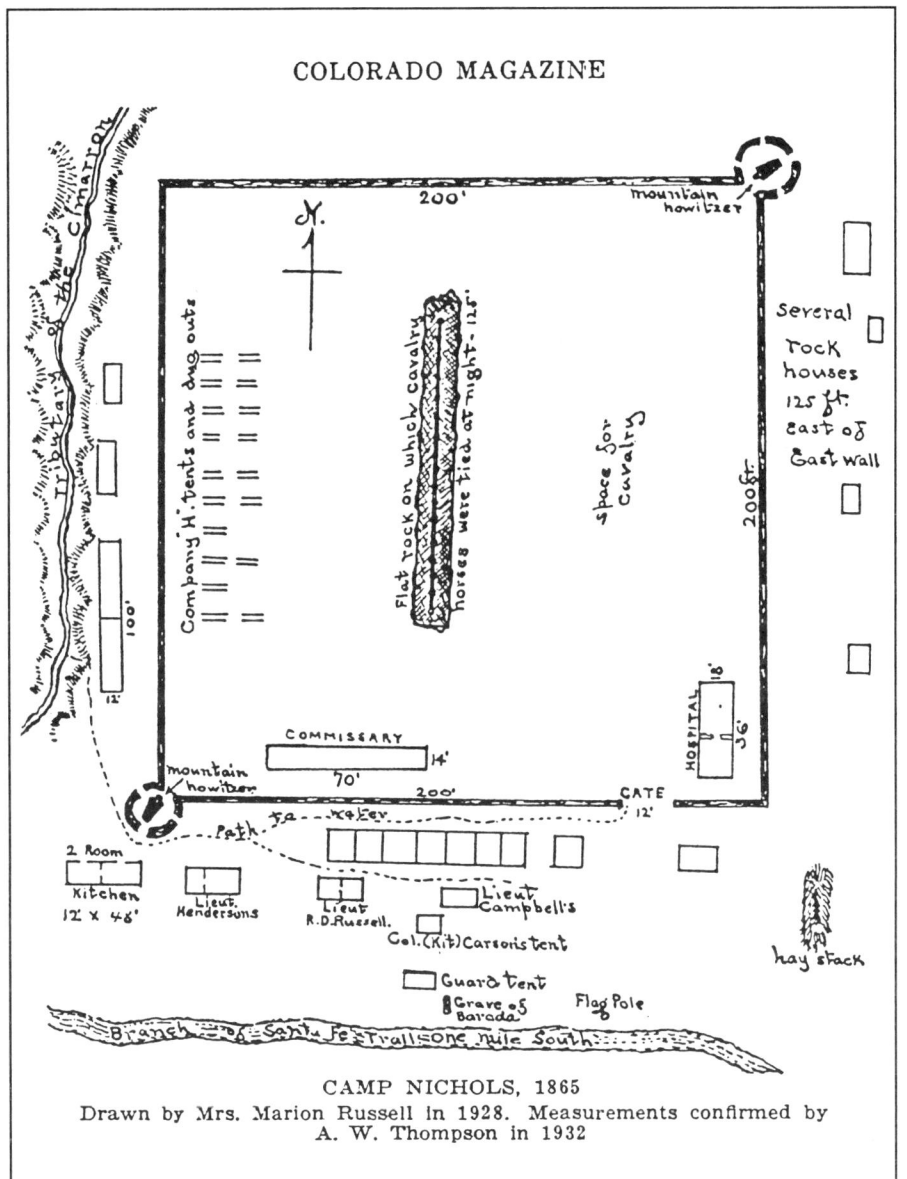

CAMP NICHOLS, 1865
Drawn by Mrs. Marion Russell in 1928. Measurements confirmed by
A. W. Thompson in 1932

Camp Nichols, Oklahoma 1935 *(Denver Public Library)*

Spring at Camp Nichols

Eliza at Camp Nichols

the exhausting forces of nature. And I could understand why man has always sought to make his presence clear and his impact strong rather than seeking to harmonize and blend with nature. It was as though nature with its greater strength and importance could always undo man and his works at a moment's notice. Nature was like an encroaching tide, steadily pushing against man, gently exerting against him a force both subtle and inexorable; though he could decisively reverse its dominance with great exertion, it would only be temporary, for collectively his powers were too weak and individually his death was assured; such were the forces of nature that they could eventually drown all his efforts.

After our reconnoiter of Camp Nichols the rest of the day was an anticlimax. The trails had increased in number through this region, and we were not able to stay with one we were sure was the main Trail. Managing to get lost we struck a course west towards the Rabbit Ears. By late afternoon we reached a road which we knew had to be one of two possible, although each was in a different state. The one in Oklahoma would go to Mexoma and the one in New Mexico would lead to Moses, just north of McNee's crossing. I did not think we had traveled far enough to be in New Mexico and I thought I recognized the country as that which I'd been through before; but when we rode on, we entered a large valley which I did not recognize. So we decided to return to the road and ask directions of some passing car. We stopped a couple and asked them what must have seemed an improbable question, "What state are we in?" They responded that we were in New Mexico, some dozen miles from Kenton, Oklahoma. This was good news for us because it meant we were only about five miles from McNee's crossing where we had left the car. We hastened on. In a few minutes the car returned and gave us the exact distance to Moses. How easy it was for them!

We were tired and the horses were exhausted so we walked and rode alternately. After what seemed an interminable period, we reached the Moses curve and saw the Trail coming in from Oklahoma and dropping over the hill to the crossing. How could we have missed it by so much? Thinking we were almost there we hurried over the hill to the spectacular slope above the crossing. We could see the dry Corrumpa below us, and the line of trees marking the abandoned town of Moses. The view ahead was dominated by the mountain called Rabbit Ears, named, we later learned, for an Indian chief rather than its profile. No sign of the farm and our car. We didn't realize then, but it lay almost nine miles ahead close to the post office called Seneca. Those last nine miles were some of the longest I can remember. The horses were too tired to carry us so we walked them for mile after mile. Each hill we topped we expected to be there; but each revealed a further stretch of road. But walking in front of our loaded horses through the abundant grasslands was novel and strangely exhilarating. Off to our left a herd of antelope drifted parallel to us, stopping to look inquiringly as they browsed in the late sun. Our pace became a measured plod, as we picked up one foot at a time and put it down. The miles slowly passed. And I took out my harmonica to augment the rhythm and soothe the animals with a melodic sense of purpose. Making up the tune, I gradually codified our pace and we came to share another theme in our endeavor.

At last the sun dropped below the horizon and as the darkness descended upon us, we came at last to the little tree-shaded lane which led up to Willy Mock's house where we would find a few days' rest and restoration. We had covered another 60 miles in the three days since we had left the Willow Bar, and we and the horses had reached the peak of condition which we were to maintain the rest of the trip.

The country we were in was dry and bushy although recent rains had improved the pasture. McNees crossing is located about twenty-four miles north and a little east of Clayton, New Mexico. The creek's name has been changed to Corrumpa and State Highway 18 crosses the creek almost at the site. A dirt road leads into the bend where the separate sets of tracks running in from the north and from the east drop down to ford the sandy bed. The ruts are clear and they join near a stone monument which states that here the first celebration of the fourth of July in present Union country was celebrated in 1831. This was the Republic of Mexico when Josiah Gregg recorded the observance in his journal. The marker stands on the old campground, a grassy flat formed by a bow in the creek. It was apparently in this same field that Indians surprised McNees and Monroe in 1828, creating the events which reputedly resulted in the Indian harassment along the Trail for the next forty years.

Gregg describes the incident:

"Two young men named McNee and Monroe, having carelessly lain down to sleep on the banks of a stream since known as McNee's Creek, were barbarously shot with their own guns, as it was supposed, in very sight of the caravan. When their comrades came up they found McNee lifeless and the other almost expiring. In this state the latter was carried nearly forty miles to the Cimarron River, where he died and was buried according to the custom of the prairies. Just as the funeral ceremonies were about to be concluded six or seven Indians appeared on the opposite side of the Cimarron. Some of the party proposed inviting them to a parley, while the rest, burning for revenge, evinced a desire to fire upon them at once. It more than probable, however, that the Indians were not only innocent but ignorant of the outrage that had been committed, or they would hardly have ventured to approach the caravan. Being quick of perception they very soon saw the belligerent attitude assumed by some of the company and therefore wheeled 'round and attempted to escape. One shot was fired, which wounded a horse and brought the Indian to the ground; when he was instantly riddled with balls. Almost simultaneously another discharge of several guns followed by which all the rest were either killed or mortally wounded except one, who escaped to bear his tribe the news of their dreadful catastrophe.

"These wanton cruelties had a most disastrous effect upon the prospects of the trade; for the exasperated children of the desert became more and more hostile to the pale faces, against whom they continued to wage a cruel war for many successive years. In fact, this same party suffered very severely a few days afterwards. They were pursued by the enraged company of the slain savages to the Arkansas River, where they were robbed of nearly a thousand head of mules and horses. But the Indians were not yet satisfied. Having beset a company of about twenty men who followed shortly after, they killed one of their number and subsequently took from them all the animals they had in their possession. The unfortunate band were now not only compelled to advance on foot, but were even constrained to carry nearly a thousand dollars each upon their backs to the Arkansas River, where it was cached (concealed in the ground) till a conveyance was procured to transfer it to the United States."[28]

Three years previous to this on October 11, 1825, the U.S. survey party of Sibley and Brown camped on the same spot and gave the creek a different name:

". . . arrived at a Creek, in the bed of which found a Pond of good Water at some distance below 2 green trees, and camped for the day, having traveled 12 Miles. Here we found very good Grass and plenty of Drift Wood. This Creek somewhat resembles the Semerone; it is in a deep Valley, and is frequently lost in Sand. Saw no trees on it except the two noted above, tho' from the great piles of Drift Wood seen, it must be well timbered above, and from the Water marks I should Judge it to be a formidable Creek at some seasons. Its general Course is from No. W. to South E. It forks just above our Camp.

"A considerable party of People left this place this Morning, and to judge from appearances, left in some haste. We suppose they are Hunters from the nearest Spanish Settlements; and I think it probable they have been hunting on the Semerone. They may have taken alarm at our Party and are hastening home in supposition that they are pursued by Indians. This is all conjecture, however. Upon some fragments of old Clothing which some of our People picked up, there were some *body lice* found, which circumstances confirmed us all in the belief that the camp had been occupied by Spaniards. We took the precaution to Pitch our Tents at a respectful distance from the old Camp. The Creek having no name, we now gave it the name of *Louse Camp Creek*."[29]

Drawing a profile of the country ahead Sibley identified the Rabbit Ears on the south, "the Mound we are steering to" (Mt. Dora south of Mt. Clayton, not yet in view), and a white top mountain (Sierra Grande) on the north. In three days they would turn and approach Mt. Clayton.

McNees crossing

Eroded Trail ruts

6 ∞ Living in Two Worlds

Our days of respite at the Mock's place was a pleasant interlude after the physical drain of Trail duties. We had breakfasts of eggs and fresh milk, shelter and comforts we had forsaken for the past two weeks, time to relax and play the guitar—even one night in a bed, although I found that my most pleasant sleep now came on the ground and preferably outside. Willy was a schoolteacher in Colorado Springs, raised in these parts and back for summer employment on the family ranch. With his wife and two girls he had taken up residence in one of the fine old stone farm houses which usually stood empty due to the continuing desertion of the land.

Providing barn and pasture for our animals, Willy viewed our activities with a sort of bemused puzzlement. Engaged as we were in further preparations and planning, our mild hubbub and vague comings and goings had a novel impact upon the household routine which seemed until then to consist of Willy's milking the cow before departing for his uncle's fields, as well as catching mice. The mouse trapping was a family ritual accomplished with the aid of a medieval-looking tin labyrinth designed to use no bait, apparently appealing instead to the rodent's quest for intellectual challenge and his scent for social amenities. The mice were drowned and the triumph was added to the score card which hung in the kitchen. This bucolic substitute for the *New York Times* and the L.A. Angels introduced us to the new day and provided an outlet for our harmless aggressions. At the time I think the tabulation was soaring over a hundred and effectively served to shame the *pelado* cats.

Our preparations included retrieving the truck and moving the car down the route, having the horses shod, and picking up some supplies in Clayton. In the process Jack went by the hospital to get some medicine for his infected leg and aching gout. At the hospital we saw a middle class black family from Texas getting an evasive rejection of medical aid at the hands of a team of receptionists who couldn't have been more interested in our own activities. It reminded me that even though we looked a bit coarse and unkempt, with outdoor long hair and scratchy beards, we still had one shining asset which is difficult to abuse: we had white skin. And I felt ashamed that I was unable to think of anything of a personal sort to rectify or even acknowledge the pathos of discrimination.

Later that day we started east towards Kansas to collect the truck; I turned to Jack and said, "Well, there's one day's travel," and in a few minutes, "There's another." It seemed incredible that all the efforts we had exerted to go these distances paled by our rapid speed back over the course, and I marveled once again at the fantastic energy at my fingertips. When we arrived at Tuttle's feed lot, the boys working there announced that the truck had been left unlocked! My camera, long lens, radio, Martin guitar and other valuables had all been sitting out for the last ten days. Locking the truck was the last thing I had mentioned to Jack before we left, and he had overlooked it. Fortunately, they had been checking it and everything was all right (an ethical legacy from the past)! While Jack drove the truck to Willow Bar for the rest of our outfit, I headed back for Seneca to meet the blacksmith coming out to shoe the horses. (Red had lost a shoe somewhere between Fort Nichols and the border.) As I drove west out of Boise City, the sky darkened to the north and an ominous storm percolated along the entire fifty-mile front before me. The dusky light turned into a deep blood red all across the grassy surface, now contrasted beneath the somber, massive sky above. Here and there gray slopes of rain connected the earth to the dark colossus poised above it. Everywhere record rains were falling; when I returned, sheets of water were thrashing around the darkened house as wind, rain, and lightning thundered in a blinding deluge. It was good fortune that we had not come in a day later.

I reached the house about 8:30, having taken six hours to cover twice the 110 miles from Lower Springs, which we had ridden over the last nine days. My present mobility, which made distances melt away and afforded heat and music at my beckoning, made me realize that I was in a different world. In terms of my recent wishes, technology had made me a god! Those sharp and constant wants had dissipated into a memory of vague and formless appetites no longer relevant.

Wednesday, as showers continued sporadically we drove to Point of Rock, New Mexico, near the site of the old Dorsey mansion. A distance of some 55 miles, it would be an easy three-day ride. The Dorsey home is an exotic combination of pioneer log cabin and sculptured stone with carved statuary on the building and the remains of a lagoon nearby. Rising starkly beside the hills, and overseeing miles of beautiful grassland, it was once the head of a vast ranch owned or controlled by a Missouri senator. Built over a period of 10 years in the 1870s, some of its furnishings were imported from Europe. Its owner is reputed to have been a thriving swindler who constructed post offices in imaginary towns on his place in order to collect a government subsidy. In a cattle trade he was reputed to have told his men to drive the herd in a circle around a hill, while the unsuspecting buyer stood by counting the magnitude of his purchase. So innocent was the purchaser that he did not even notice one conspicuous cow which kept reappearing at regular intervals, and had to be yanked out of the procession to keep it looking legitimate.

We had intended to leave the next morning after resting the horses for two days, but when we woke up, the sky was overcast and there was an off again, on again drizzle. We tried to saddle up and pack the horses

Original part of Dorsey mansion

"Conspicuous consumption"

between sporadic bursts, but soon it started to rain harder. After being comfortable and dry, it was impossible to go out and deliberately get soaked at the very start of a day's journey. So we sat around all morning watching the sky for some sign of improvement. After days of constant thirst and oppressive heat, this definitely represented a new phase of our experience. Finally, the sky lightened up to where we thought it was worth chancing a departure, and leaving shelter and comfort behind, we embarked once again. We passed several miles to the north of Rabbit Ears mountain (in the very early days, the road was to the south, but by the time Gregg wrote, this way was out of use). A light drizzle fell as we followed the deep ruts down a slope to the Alamos (cottonwood) Creek where the old Turkey Creek camping ground had been located. Near here in 1836 Gregg met the Mexican *Ciboleros*, or buffalo hunters, and learned of the death of Jedediah Smith:

"A word concerning the *Ciboleros* may not be altogether uninteresting. Every year large parties of New Mexicans, some provided with mules and asses, others with *carretas* or trucklecarts and oxen, drive out into these prairies to procure a supply of buffalo beef for their families. They hunt like the wild Indians, chiefly on horseback and with bow and arrow, or lance, with which they soon load their carts and mules. They find no difficulty in curing their meat even in mid summer, by slicing it thin and spreading or suspending it in the sun; or, if in haste, it is slightly barbecued. During the curing operation they often follow the Indian practice of beating or kneading the slices with their feet, which they contend contributes to the preservation."[30]

We rode 15 miles that afternoon and camped by a spectacular metamorphic rock outcropping in the pasture of Louise Cook, about six miles east of the old Rabbit Ears camp. Pools of water lay beneath the jagged cliff face which overlooked a small arroyo. The rock was a natural camp and loose stone had been piled along one face of the slab making a small pen. We set up our tent on the lee side of the rock. Twenty feet away was a perfect circle of rocks about 12 feet in diameter. At first I was puzzled as to what it was. Being so symmetrical, it had to be man made. Looking around at the rich grass in the small protected pasture, I realized that this perfect camp site had been used by Indians, and these distinct remains were a tipi ring—the rocks anchoring the base of the tent and enclosing a fire pit. Of the dozen or more such remains on this stretch of the plains, this was the clearest and most perfect I saw. In my mind I could reconstruct how hunting parties, riding up the small draw, would stop at the pools below the cliff. From behind it one could easily walk up the gradual slope to the top for a good view in both directions, and below and behind the rock, one would be out of sight and protected from the prevailing winds. Perhaps the Indians had constructed the walls to hold their grazing ponies.

That night torrential rains fell. We had brought the small tent because of the threatening weather, but tonight even it failed to keep out the soaking downpour. In the middle of the night Jack woke me to tell me he was freezing and wanted into my bag. He had been lying in a low spot which had accumulated runoff coming down the slope and he was now four inches deep in water. His bag had flooded and his clothes were wet; the tent walls, which were coated with moisture, were beginning to drop onto his head and legs. I was situated on a little island, but my boots, camera, and other "possibles" were floating just off shore. We huddled on the high spot trying not to move and lower the bag into the rising water.

Even though we were on the side of a hill, the volume of runoff striking the tent was such that we might as well have been on level ground. All night we lay there listening to the thunder and analyzing shifts in wind and the beating of drops to decide if the storm was going to let up or persist, threatening to engulf us. I felt pretty lucky so far. I had originally placed my things on Jack's side, but he had specified that he wanted to sleep on that spot so I had grumbled a little and moved my things. Now I was the only dry creature in all of outdoor Union county. Jack's ability to "tune out" was a definite advantage now as he lay there shivering, the moisture aggravating his gout. I had covered the saddles with the tarp and taken a walk in the intermittent moonlight before going to bed. Now there was nothing to do but wait until morning and hope we got enough sun to dry things out.

This morning, Friday, July 21st, dawned partly cloudy and we were able to get things dry enough to pack. We headed towards Round Mound and nooned during the heat of the day at another abandoned ranch. I had one of those fantastic tuna sandwiches and then rode across the rough lava flats, towards the Grenville road. On the trail out of the stream bottom and up onto the mesa we could see where wagon wheels had worn grooves into the rock as they topped the hill. From his diary, I remember that Sibley had reached this place Friday, October 14th, 1825. This must have been a tough stretch for wagons. There was a historical marker where we crossed the railroad tracks, and people in passing cars waved as we rode briefly along the highway. Turning in towards the Mound the weather started to cloud up badly. By the time we reached the base, a driving rain had begun and we started to look for shelter. We saw a dilapidated house about a mile north of us with a barn on the other side, and we headed for it in a run. About that time a bolt of lightning crashed to the ground in that direction, and we had to stop and open two gates to get into the field. Red began to act confused. He didn't know who he was racing and didn't want to run. He began twisting sideways and slowing down. Another bolt of lightning, this time between us and the barn. I kicked him with the spurs and he jumped forward. A large herd of antelope was racing in an oblique path beside us as I continued to kick him and shout, leaning forward over his head.

The lightning was crashing overhead now, and I began to get scared. Jack was racing behind me without a coat as the rain poured down. I crouched low in the saddle pretending I was ducking the menacing flashes. In my mind I began to go over the people I had known who'd been killed by lightning. Only a quarter mile now, if we could just avoid being struck. The barn door was open and birds and cattle scattered as we ducked down and raced through the opening. Inside it was large and dry and cushioned in cowshit. We unsaddled our panting mounts and went to the doorway to watch the show.

The next three hours we witnessed the most incredible display of pyrotechnics I have ever experienced. It began with the same blood red sunset I had seen coming out of Oklahoma, the grass golden and the silhouettes of animals glowing in the declining sun. The show culminated in hours of lightning rolling and flashing above the lofty accumulated clouds. I stood there in paroxysms of joy as the light rolled across the billowing underside of the sky. Summer storms have always fascinated me anyway, but this was like something from another world. Above, the clouds' reflection lighted thunderheads into a translucent volume. The lightning would begin far off to the west and race towards me, tracing an illuminated route on the cloud's underside. Below, gaps between the storms sent shafts of light radiating towards the earth, jumping and darting in different directions as the electricity tore the sky. It was as though separate frames of film had been juxtaposed without an interval to explain each new position to the eye. Streaking, flashing, bursting on the ground, the bolts of lightning continued. Far to the west, to Point of Rocks where we would ride, the whole country was blazing in splendor. Exhausted at last, I had to give up watching and roll into my bed, trying to keep my eyes open as long as possible to enjoy the drama for just one more burst. It was one of the awesome experiences of my life. Still, I fell asleep.

A beautiful clear morning and I remained dazzled by that display of last night. We passed Mt. Clayton wishing we could take the time to climb it, but feeling now that we wanted to push on. There are a lot of buffalo wallows in the area; and when we stopped at an old house to get directions, the fellow told us that they find a lot of arrowheads in them. Makes sense—a good place to hunt buffalo. The country is rolling and grassy, and we play tag with two herds of antelope all morning. At one point Big Red starts to go down on his knees. It takes me completely by surprise and I think he's going to roll over on me—a bad habit he's probably picked up from Linda. I jump off. But he doesn't roll, I think he just wants to get rid of some of the flies which are thick and pesky due to the rain. We seem finally to be leaving tortoise country, for I haven't seen the tiny ladder tracks for a while now. We run into another rattlesnake which Jack shoots. Here Gregg observed:

> "At last some of the most persevering of our adventurers succeeded in ascending the summit of the Round Mound, which commands a full and advantageous view of the surrounding country, in some directions to the distance of a hundred miles or more. Looking southward, a varied country is seen, of hills, plains, mounds, and sandy undulations; but on the whole northern side extensive plains spread out, studded occasionally with variegated peaks and ridges. Far beyond these to the northwestward, and low in the horizon, a silvery stripe appears upon an azure base resembling a list of chalk-white clouds. This is the perennially snow-capped summit of the eastern spur of the Rocky Mountains.
>
> "These immense bordering plains and even the hills with which they are interspersed are wholly destitute of timber, except a chance scattering tree upon the margins of the bluffs and ravines, which but scantily serves to variegate the landscape. Not even a buffalo was now to be seen to relieve the dull monotony of the scene; although at some seasons (and particularly in the fall) literally strewed with herds of this animal. . . .
>
> "As the caravan was passing under the northern base of the Round Mound it presented a very fine and imposing spectacle to those who were upon its summit. The wagons marched slowly in four parallel columns, but in broken lines, often at intervals of many rods between. The unceasing crack, crack, of the wagoners' whips, resembling the frequent reports of distant guns, almost made one believe that a skirmish was actually taking place between two hostile parties: and a hostile engagement it virtually was to the poor brutes, at least; for the merciless application of the whip would sometimes make the blood spurt from their sides—and that often without any apparent motive of the wanton *carrettieri,* other than to amuse themselves with the flourishing and loud popping of their lashes!
>
> "The rear wagons are usually left without a guard; for all the loose horsemen incline to be ahead, where they are to be seen moving in scattered groups, some times a mile or more in advance. As our camp was pitched but a mile west of the Round Mound, those who lingered upon its summit could have an interesting view of the evolutions of 'forming' the wagons, in which the drivers by this time had become very expert. When marching four abreast, the two exterior lines spread out and then meet at the front angle; while the two inner lines keep close together until they reach the point of the rear angle, when they wheel suddenly out and close with the hinder ends of the other two; thus

systematically concluding a right-lined quadrangle, with a gap left at the rear corner for the introduction of the animals.

"Our encampment was in a beautiful plain, but without water, of which, however, we had a good supply at noon. Our cattle, as was the usual custom, after having grazed without for a few hours, were now shut up in the pen of the wagons. Our men were all wrapt in peaceful slumber, except the guard, who kept their silent watch around the encampment; when all of a sudden, about the ominous hour of midnight, a tremendous uproar was heard, which caused every man to start in terror from his blanket couch with arms in hand. Some animal, it appeared, had taken fright at a dog and by a sudden start set all around him in violent motion: the panic spread simultaneously throughout the pen; and a scene of rattle, clash, and lumbering ensued which far surpassed everything we had yet witnessed. A general stampede (*estampida*, as the Mexicans say) was the result. Notwithstanding the wagons were tightly bound together, wheel to wheel, with ropes or chains, and several stretched across the gaps at the corners of the *corral*, the oxen soon burst their way out; and though mostly yoked in pairs, they went scampering over the plains, as though Tam O'Shanter's cutty-sark Nannie had been at their tails. All attempts to stop them were vain; for it would require Auld Clootie himself to check the headway of a drove of oxen when once thoroughly frightened. Early the following morning we made active exertions to get up a sufficient quantity of teams to start the caravan. At Rock Creek, a distance of six or seven miles, we were joined by those who had gone in pursuit of the stock. All the oxen were found except some half a dozen, which were never recovered. No mules were lost: a few that had broken through were speedily retaken. The fact is that though mules are generally easiest scared, oxen are decidedly the worst when once started. The principal advantage of the latter in this respect is that Indians have but little inducement to steal them, and therefore few attempts would be made upon a caravan of oxen. We were now entering a region of rough, and in some places rocky, road, as the streams which intervene from this to the mountains are all bordered with fine sand stone. These rugged passes acted very severely upon our wagons, as the wheels were by this time becoming loose and shackling, from the shrink of the wood occasioned by the extreme dryness and rarity of this elevated atmosphere. The spokes of some were beginning to reel in the hubs, so that it became necessary to brace them with false spokes, firmly bound with buffalo tug. On some occasions the wagon tires have become so loose upon the felloes as to tumble off while traveling. The most effective mode of tightening slackened tires (at least that most practiced on the plains, as there is rarely a portable forge in company), is by driving strips of hoop-iron around between the tire and felloe—simple wedges of wood are sometimes made to supply the place of iron. During halts I have seen a dozen wheels being repaired at the same time, occasioning such a clitter clatter of hammers that one would almost fancy himself in a shipyard.

"Emerging from this region of asperities, we soon passed the Point of Rocks, as a diminutive spur projecting from the north is called, at the foot of which springs a charming little fount of water. This is but thirty or forty miles from the principal mountains, along whose border similar detached ridges and hills are frequently to be seen. The next day, having descended from the table-plain, we reached the principal branch of the Canadian River, which is here but a rippling brook hardly a dozen paces in width, though eighty miles from its source in the mountains to the north. The bottom being of solid rock, this ford is appropriately called by the Ciboleros *El Vado de Piedras*. The banks are very low and easy to ascend. The stream is called *Río Colorado* by its literal translation of Red River. This circumstance perhaps gave rise to the belief that it was the head branch of our main stream of this name: but the nearest waters of the legitimate Red River of Natchitoches are still a hundred miles to the south of this road.

"In descending to the *Río Colorado* we met a dozen or more of our countrymen from Taos, to which town (sixty or seventy miles distant there is a direct but rugged route across the mountains. It was a joyous encounter for among them we found some of our old acquaintances whom we had not seen for many years. During our boyhood we had spelled together in the same country school."[31]

Matt Field[5] tells a humorous story which occurred somewhere in this region on his way back from Santa Fe in 1839:

"It was two hours past noon and two men were alone upon the prairie. Save these two human beings, the only things of life within view were a wounded buffalo cow in the next hollow of the prairie, and an old grey mare, that was *staked* (fastened by a long halter to a stick driven into the ground) in the hollow where the men were crouching.

"'Don't waste another shot, Tom, the old cow is done for.'

"'Waste shot!—but you don't consider how much time we are wasting. It's four hours since the wagons passed us, and they are now fifteen miles ahead.'

"'Ain't that your last charge?'

"'To be sure it is, and here it goes plump into the old cow's liver.'

"'Stop, stop, Tom—now, for heaven's sake, keep that charge.' The cow was seen to drop upon her knees. 'There, you see the work is done; I am reduced to my last shot too, and if any of those Camanches or Pawnees should—'

"The speaker was interrupted by a roar of loud and unrestrained laughter. 'Well, Sam,' said Tom, 'I do despise a coward, and if you ain't a perfect fenomenon of that genus I'm the handle of a tea-pot. Once, twice—going, going—look at the old cow roll over now, will you?'

"'Tom, stop,' said Sam, laying his hand upon his comrade's rifle and lowering the muzzle to the grass. 'Now, you must keep that shot; the cow will be dead in ten minutes, and we'll have time to butcher and get the meat and reach camp before dark.'

"'You! That buffalo will get up when she's done saying her prayers and be out of sight in a jiffy, if I don't pop her over. Let go.'

"'Sam, I ask it as a favor. Will you just remember where we are, and only two of us?—God heavens, the Camanches,—'

"'D—n the Camanches! How do they know whether a fellow's gun is loaded or not? Any ten of them will run from an American rifle if there was a grain of powder in it. Sit down, Sammy, there's a good boy.'

"Tom was upon his knees, and using his ramrod for a rest, he took deliberate aim at the dying cow.

"'Tom, you're a fool,' said Sam.

"'Sam, you're a Sammy,' said Tom. 'O Sammy, Sammy, think of your anxious mammy'—Click—bang! and as the shot sped the hunter threw himself prostrate upon his face, and without looking at his companion, he exclaimed in a voice strangely changed from gaiety to alarm, 'For God's sake, Sam, what is that?'

"Sam gave a swift glance around the prospect and instantly dropped to the earth in imitation of his companion.

"'Sam! Sam! What is that?' said Tom, in a voice so altered from its former merry vaunting tone that it scarcely seemed to belong to the same individual.

"'Indians! there are five at least, and heaven knows how many more behind,' said Sam, placing a fresh cap upon his rifle, and then adding, 'Have you not another charge?'

"'Gracious heaven, no,' said Tom, 'I have powder, but my last ball is gone.'

"'Take this,' said Sam, taking a bullet from his mouth, where it had lain to create moisture for his parched throat. 'Load.'

"'Father of Heaven, Sam, do you think—'

"'Load!' said Sam, in an imperative yet calm tone; and Tom remembered that a minute before he had called Sam a coward.

"While Tom proceeded to re-load Sam raised himself cautiously from the ground to reconnoitre the coming danger.

"'Do you see them, Sam? Are they coming toward us?'

"'Not precisely in this direction,' replied Sam; 'we might perhaps escape, but they must have heard your shot.'

"'O Sam, that shot! O, if I hadn't fired! I'll never fire another shot, Sam never! Never!'

"Poor Tom had a heart made all for love and kindness; any girl might have won a treasure in it and prized it greatly, yet was it now a thing of less value than five grains of powder.

"'There is a large party,' said Sam, still observing, 'I can count fifteen spear heads glancing in the sun beam.'

"Tom groaned.

"'Yet they are not coming this way.'

"'What!' said Tom, lifting his head. 'But the old mare. Ah, they will see the old grey beast and there's no avoiding it.'

"'Oh, the confounded old beast! O, Sam, must we be killed for an old horse! Well, now, d—n that old horse, it never was good for any thing either. O Sam, can't you coax it to lay down? Betsy! Poor old Betsy! Lay down, you d——d old horse, lay down!'

"Poor old Betsy was innocently grazing some forty feet from where the two hunters were, and paid not the slightest attention to Tom's kind entreaties.

"Suddenly Sam dropped again precipitately by the side of Tom.

"'Are they coming?' whispered Tom in an unearthly voice, as he buried his face in the grass.

"'Hush—listen!' said Sam, placing his fingers upon the lock of his rifle.

"Hoof steps rapidly approaching were now distinctly heard beating hollowly over the level earth. Tears rushed from poor Tom's eyes the instant this sound reached his ear.

"'Cock your rifle,' said Sam, sternly.

"'I can't—I can't Sam; shoot it yourself. O I'm a dead man. I haven't been married a year, Sam, and my mother loves me more than any of the other boys! O Mary, God bless you! you'll never see me again. To die, and be scalped, and shot, and killed by Camanches!—red devils!—where there aint a tree nor a drop of water!

"'O mother, mother, if I was with you at home again I'd never leave you, never, never, never!'

"Two or three shots were now heard, and poor Tom continued, never raising his face from the grass, 'Yes, there they go—some big Camanche has got his gun leveled at me now. Good-by, mother! Good-by, Mary! Are you dead yet, Sam? Good-by! God bless you! Yes I'm a dead man, and my hair is gone. O Sam, Sam, how the wolves will knock our bones about!'

"Tom was now completely alone, Sam having crept away into the next hollow to observe more nearly the horse men, who he could now perceive were in chase of the poor wounded cow which had sprang up and ran toward them when pierced by Tom's last ball. Thus poor Tom lay in solitary despair mourning and bewailing his fate, when a single rider came at full speed directly to the spot where he was lying. Tom heard the horsemen rein in his steed, and his voice became mute, his breath seemed to leave his body and his heart to cease its action.

"'Why, friend, are you dead or asleep?' said the rider.

"Had the expected ball pierced his heart, Tom could not have changed his position more suddenly. He sprang from his face into a sitting posture, and after rubbing his eyes, wet with tears, with his hands, which were black with powder, he sat gazing at the horseman with a mingled expression of utter amazement and unbelieving joy.

"'Wha-a-a-at?' was the only word he could make out to utter.

"'Why, my friend, why aint you butchering that cow over there? Those Spaniards will have all your meat away from you.'

"'Spaniards!' almost shrieked Tom, as he sprang to his feet and looked in the direction pointed to by the stranger.

"A glance was enough for Tom. He saw a crowd of men round the dead cow, but not one of them looked like an Indian. He turned to the stranger beside him and saw a man dressed in garments which betokened him from the States, and speaking his own language; and with a jump in the air and a loud shout of joy he rushed to the horseman, grasping his hands and embracing his legs and his horses neck with every extravagant demonstration of overflowing delight." (pp.273-277)

Jaffa at buffalo wallow

Around noon we began to wonder where we were. There were many tracks to follow and none were too clear. We had a detailed section map but the intermittent nature of the tracks led us off the Trail twice in the last three days.

Now as we looked south towards the Don Carlos Hills (named for the commander in a big victory over the Comanches "many years ago"— according to Sibley in 1825), we decided to head for the town of Sofia to get directions and some grain for the horses. Sofia is one of those contemporary depopulated towns which can't make up its mind if it wants to be a village or just a big ranch. It used to have a railroad, school, stores, etc., which are now abandoned, and the big buildings have been turned into houses or stand empty. We stopped at a modern-looking ranch house surrounded by tall cottonwoods and asked the woman if she could spare some feed for our horses. She looked very indecisive and told us to ask her husband who was down the road about five miles baling some hay or something. We explained that a ride like that is the better part of a day for us, and she caught onto our situation. She was actually quite friendly after her initial reserve, and had some kind of European accent. Pretty soon her husband returned—he was foreman for the outside corporation which owns all of this country—and he immediately set us up with goodies to eat, drink, maps, etc. He told us that the real Round Mound is a hill south of town (a dispute between history books we have encountered elsewhere) and told us a little about the country. He had only recently moved there but the town was settled by Bulgarians early in the century. He also told us that a woman was killed by lightning while riding horseback off in the direction we came from and that six cattle were killed on the high plains towards Point of Rock where we were going.

In the meantime the horses had gotten loose and wandered down the road in search of better grazing and equine companionship. A truck drove up and told us that they were down by the next gate rolling around like they had the Holy Ghost. When we got to them they and all our baggage were covered with dust. Of course, I had my camera with me now that Red had finally picked up Linda's inspiration, and I opened the saddlebag to find the pieces of the lens cover rattling around in the plastic sack like so many BB's. I was so mad I was about ready to ventilate him with the toe of my boot. As I cursed him roundly he summoned his deepest look of bedraggled idiocy, poised between utter unintelligence, hurt, and pathos, his eyes proclaiming, "How can you say these awful things about me? I don't understand what you mean," this giving way to a twitch of fear as I moved towards him menacingly to show him just what I did mean. We left it at that for now, "but if I catch you doing that again. . . ."

And so we headed out again along a dusty gravel road leading due west. The country was changing now from impressive to spectacular. To the north the beautiful symmetry of the Sierra Grande seemed to float like a mirage above the surface of the plain. To the west of the Sierra, parallel to our course, the low, broken line of the foothills formed a craggy wall leading west some forty miles to the jagged spine of the Rocky Mountains. The view was even enough to inspire faint praise from Sibley, for whom most of the trip seemed to have lain somewhere between a chore and an imposition. The afternoon was dead-still; in the calm you could almost feel the quiet sounds of land in heat, insects, and air through your body, not even needing your ears. And the view was stunning. Rolling mesas and prairie climb gradually towards the front hills on my right. Rising and falling ahead, they seemed infinite but for the breaking action of the cloud-like peaks off in the distance. Above a turbulent sky contrasted with the graceful landscape, adding dark patches of shadow to the northern hills. The scene inspired in me a feeling of awe and contentment. It was a quiet joy, yet excitement stirred inside as the secret, futile wish arose: if only I could hold the feeling of this instant to draw it out when needed. But I could only look and see what is before me and take my chances with the memory. And it was enough.

Now it was beginning to darken. Clouds were flooding down from the mountains in a huge black mist and cooling us as they blocked out the summer sun. A pickup truck came down the road towards us, and stopped.

"How much for those Mexican spurs?" one of them asked.

"Thanks, but not for sale," I answered.

"You boys have any way to get out of the rain?" they asked.

"We have ponchos," I answered. (At least I did; Jack never got around to buying one.)

"You're gonna be needin' 'em." They waved and drove off as we turned from the road and crossed down into a valley, then climbed up onto a broad plateau which extends as far as the sprawling mountain. By now the iron gray cloud of rain which had been drifting down out of the foothills had been replaced by a broad storm containing lightning, thunder and, judging by the dark sweeping pouches hanging down from under the thunderhead, a measure of hail, as well. I thought of the story we had just heard in Sofia. Last week a fellow east of town had been caught in the hail and couldn't find shelter. His horse fought hard and broke away from him as the hail pulverized his body, driving all the blood into his legs until the veins burst. He had been in the hospital since, unable to walk. I speculated on just how much of my body I could squeeze under a saddle as a light rain began to fall.

"Maybe we'd better look for a cave." But we push ahead, on the mesa now as the storm suddenly swept down on us. The rain was driving, and the lightning began to crash around us. We were the tallest thing for a mile. Goddam, that storm moved fast! "We've got to run for it, Jack, and get off this mesa before we get killed!" It was pouring so hard we couldn't hear each other. There was a large canyon with trees in it and a house about two miles north and west of us, and we could see a road leading across the mesa which dropped over the side into the canyon. "Let's make it to that canyon." We tried to run, but the wind was so strong it held us back and the rain was practically horizontal as we forced the horses into it. Lightning crashed somewhere on the mesa behind us. Red jumped as I spurred him in the flank and lashed him with the reins. Half a mile to the rim. Jack was somewhere beside me but I couldn't turn my head without losing my hat. On we raced as the lightning increased its intensity. This splendid place was going to kill us! The rain began to mix with hail and the lightning hissed as it cracked around us. The storm was still increasing its furor as we reached a fence and gate at the edge. (What a time to have to open a gate!)

The road cut down the side of the mesa and at its side the gully had washed deep from previous rains. We got off the horses and herded them into the gully ducking down from the lightning. I tied a long lead to Red so we were not too close to each other. The rain was beating down now, mixed with hail. The lightning crashed down at the top of the hill above us, first a sizzle, then an explosion followed by a rumble murmuring off into the distance. Standing in the gully my eye was at ground level, and I watched the rain and hail bouncing a foot up into the air again after striking the dirt. Looking down the gully I saw Red standing complacently, watching me, and some twenty feet beyond, only the top of Jack and the horse were visible since the force of falling rain had eliminated all visibility close to the ground. We waited in partial concealment until finally the thunder began to move on. But so much water had fallen that the gully, which started out a stream washing over the tops of my boots, had become a torrent undermining our footing. I crouched down, my feet wedged into the slimy banks on either side; but as I looked down at Red again, I could see that he was beginning to slide down the hillside. He was moving slowly, like an iceberg, and the rope was being drawn from my hand. I had to get him out of there before he was swept away! I clamored up the bank, sliding and falling as I reached the road and tried to find firm footing. I moved toward Red and said a few words to him, then began to pull on the lead rope. He struggled to move as the current clawed at his legs. Then he got his feet on the side and out he came. Jack followed him out and we waited out the rest of the storm on higher ground. Then, as suddenly as it has started, it became a gentle shower with only the distant rumble of thunder. Below us the stream in the depths of the canyon had become a flowing chocolate sea, and I called to Jack, "We had better get across that before it rises in the runoff." And we slipped and slid our way down the hill and cross the stream.

"Wow! What a storm," we said almost simultaneously. We were standing there dripping and miserable. My poncho had kept my chest and back dry, but everything else was soaked; because of the force of the rain, my pants and boots were covered with mud. About the time we turned down the road and began talking about what had happened, thunder crashed nearby and the rain began again.

"Jesus Christ, it's coming back!" Soon the torrential downpour began again, and the lightning crashed on the ground behind us. This time we were caught in the open. We let go of the horses, and I kicked off my spurs and threw them over by my horse. (I guess you know who's number one now, eh, Red?) And we crouched down as the sky fell in pieces all about us.

Half an hour later we were still alive, and the mud on my pants had been taken care of. By now we were starting to get cold, and we decided to head up to the ranch house ahead and call it a day. The road had its bank cut away and the pudding-colored water was still rushing down the sides of the surrounding hills and pouring into the barrow pit as we picked our way across the slope, testing for solid footing. The house was a luxurious-looking *adobe*, with a tall tower, walls, trees and barns in the back. We started fantasizing about just what we'd like to find there: a hot bath, a roaring fire before a great stone hearth, some dry clothes which would turn out to fit us, a tall mixed drink, and yes, a couple of young lovelies who are consummate history buffs. Leading the horses around the back of the house by the barns we saw half a dozen timorous faces bobbing around the window. (What are these strange goings on?) As we walked up to the kitchen door, everybody disappeared but one, who, remaining behind the closed door when we asked for the owner, pointed vigorously behind us with a look like maybe a puma had just consumed him and is poised to spring on the pair of us. Turning towards the barn, we saw a man coming toward us. He was middle- aged, short, looked something like a cross between Jack Benny and the short guy out of Mutt and Jeff. We exchanged a few pleasantries about the weather ("Some storm, eh?" "Sure was." etc.), and it became obvious that Armijo (for that is his name, and I'm not likely to forget it) was not a bit interested in having us stay there. ("No room in the barns," he said.) In desperation Jack asked if we could have a shot of whiskey to warm up. "Just used up the last of it, wish I had some myself." What a downer!

We headed on down the road, too wet to want the saddle. The sun was getting low in the western sky, painting the underside of the streaky clouds with a salmon light. (Where were we going to camp and find dry wood in this place?) We circled the lagoons which cover the road and remount, following the river. Coming around the point of the cliff we found our answer. There were some abandoned buildings with boards and broken furniture in them. A rabbit darted out from under a barn and stopped on the hillside. Fresh meat would be good now, and I take out my rifle to bust him in the clearing. "Plop." The dirt splattered beside him and he took off. A second shot, I couldn't see where it went, and the hare was up on a ledge directly opposite me located in the saddle. Perfect shot. "Ping! Whine! Zing!" I blasted away as the rabbit blinked at me in disbelief, obviously in no mortal danger, protected by the gulf of twenty feet between us. Then he turned and dinner disappeared into the rocks. Disgusted, I threw the gun away. "Nice shooting," comments Jack. "Sheet!!"

Second storm camp

But we had found our camp. The cliff face consisted of huge scattered chunks of stone which had broken off and left small spaces like rooms along the face. Someone had walled a few of these spaces off and lived in them, and there were passages and corrals as well. We set up a reflector and built a fire against a wall of our room. Soon we had a comfortable shelter and our clothes were drying over frames around the fireplace. The horses were hobbled down by the river and from our cozy castle above the valley, the moon afforded us a view of our one-night kingdom below. Given the experiences of the day, it was one of the finest campsites we had.

The next day we rejoined the Trail, which we left during the storm the previous afternoon. The four tracks now pointed west across the rolling plains to the famous Point of Rock (New Mexico). Somewhere near our present location one of the most frequently told incidents of the Trail's history occurred.

In October 1849, the party of a Santa Fe trader, J. M. White, with some half dozen people including his wife, ten-year-old daughter, and a colored servant, was returning from St. Louis. Anxious to reach Santa Fe, they determined that Indian danger was ended and hurried ahead of the caravan with which they had been traveling. Camping for the night a few

Ruts approaching Point of Rocks, New Mexico

miles east of Point of Rock, they were visited by a party of Jicarilla Apaches under White Wolf, apparently in alliance with Utes, who demanded gifts from the travelers. White ordered them out of camp, and when they returned later, they overturned the wagons, scalped and mutilated White and several others, and took captive Mrs. White, her daughter and servant. Shortly afterwards, a band of Pueblo Indian buffalo hunters reported seeing the captives in the Apache camp and word was relayed to the military garrison at Taos.

As Kit Carson tells the story:

"A party was organized in Taos with Leroux and Fisher as guides, to rescue them. When they reached Rayado, I was also employed as a guide. We marched to the place where the depredation had been committed, and then followed the trail of the Indians. I was the first man to discover the camp where the murder had been perpetrated. The trunks of the unfortunate family had been broken open, the harnesses cut to pieces, and everything else that the Indians could not carry away with them had been destroyed. We tracked them for ten or twelve days over the most difficult trail that I have ever followed. Upon leaving their camps they would separate in small groups of two or three persons and travel in different directions, to meet again at some appointed place. In nearly every camp we found some of Mrs. White's clothing, and these discoveries spurred us to continue the pursuit with renewed energy.

"We finally came in view of the Indian camp. I was in the advance, and at once started for it, calling to our men to come on. The commanding officer ordered a halt, however, and no one followed me. I was afterwards informed that Leroux, the principal guide, had advised the officer to halt us, as the Indians wished to have a parley. The latter, seeing that the troops did not intend to charge, commenced packing up in all haste. Just as the halt was ordered, the commanding officer was shot; the ball passed through his coat, his gauntlets that were in his pocket, and his shirt, stopping at the skin, and doing no other damage than making him a little sick at the stomach. The gauntlets had saved his life, sparing a gallant officer to the service of his country. As soon as he had recovered from the shock given him by the ball, he ordered the men to charge, but it was too late to save the captives. There was only one Indian left in the camp who was promptly shot while he was running into the river in a vain effort to escape. At a distance of about 200 yards, the body of Mrs. White was found, still perfectly warm. She had been shot through the heart with an arrow not more than five minutes before. She evidently knew that some one was coming to her rescue. Although she did not see us, it was apparent that she was endeavoring to make her escape when she received the fatal shot.

"I am certain that if the Indians had been charged immediately on our arrival, she would have been saved. They did not know of our approach, and as they were not paying any particular attention to her, perhaps she could have managed to run towards us, and if she had, the Indians would have been afraid to follow her. However, the treatment she had received from them was so brutal and horrible that she could not possibly have lived very long. Her death, I think, should never be regretted by her friends. She is surely far more happy in heaven, with her God, than among her friends on this earth.

"I do not wish to be understood as attaching any blame to the officer in command of the expedition or to the principal guide. They acted as they thought best for the purpose of saving Mrs. White. We merely differed in opinion at the time, but I have no doubt that they now see that if my advice had been taken, her life might have been saved, for at least a short period.

"We pursued the Indians for about six miles on a level prairie. We captured all their baggage and camp equipage, many of them running off without any of their clothing. We also took some of their animals. One warrior was killed, and two or three children were captured. We found a book in the camp, the first of the kind I had ever seen, in which I was represented as a great hero, slaying Indians by the hundred. I have often thought that Mrs. White must have read it, and knowing that I lived nearby, must have prayed for my appearance in order that she might be saved. I did come, but I lacked the power to persuade those that were in command over me to follow my plan for her rescue. They would not listen to me and they failed. I will say no more regarding this matter, nor attach any blame to any particular person, for I presume the consciences of those who were the cause of the tragedy have severely punished them ere this."[32]

The fate of Mrs. White was apparently typical "bride of the plains" treatment, which is to say she was passed from chief to chief. It was a fate common to adult female slaves and was so horrible that many times ransomed captives would refuse to return home and face old acquaintances after the experience. An Apache chief later commented on the massacre, telling of his attack upon Mrs. White and stating that the child had been killed on the Canadian. Even so, in 1850 the 31st Congress voted $1,000 for "redemption of the daughter of the late Mr. J. M. White now supposedly in captivity of Apaches." The case stirred special excitement among residents of the territory both because of the standing of Mr. White in the Santa Fe community and because his blond and attractive wife was highly popular among local residents.

Inman describes the end of White Wolf in what he calls the only duel between cavalry and Indians to occur on the frontier:

"The fate of the Apache chief, White Wolf, who was the leader in the outrages in the *cañon* of the Canadian, was fitting for his devilish deeds. It was Lieutenant David Bell's fortune to avenge the murder of Mrs. White and her family, and in an extraordinary manner. The action was really dramatic, or romantic; he was on a scout with his company, which was stationed at Fort Union, New Mexico, having about thirty men with him, and when near the *cañon* of the Canadian they met about the same number of Indians. A parley was in order at once, probably desired by the savages, who were confronted with an equal number of troopers. Bell had assigned the baggage mules to the care of five or six of his command, and held a mounted interview with the chief, who was no other than the infamous White Wolf of the Jicarilla Apaches. As Bell approached, White Wolf was standing in front of his Indians, who were on foot, all well armed and in perfect line. Bell was in advance of his troopers, who were about twenty paces from the Indians, exactly equal in number and extent of line; both parties were prepared to use firearms.

"The parley was almost tediously long and the impending duel was arranged, White Wolf being very bold and defiant.

"At last the leaders exchanged shots, the chief sinking on one knee and aiming his gun, Bell throwing his body forward and making his horse rear. Both lines, by command fired, following the example of their superiors, the troopers, however, spurring forward over their enemies. The warriors, or nearly all of them, threw themselves on the ground, and several vertical wounds were received by horse and rider. The dragoons turned short about, and again charged through and over their enemies, the fire being continuous. As they turned for a third charge, the surviving Indians were seen escaping to a deep ravine, which, although only one or two hundred paces off, had not previously been noticed. A number of the savages thus escaped, the troopers having to pull up at the brink, but sending a volley after the descending fugitives.

"In less than fifteen minutes twenty-one of the forty-six actors in this strange combat were slain or disabled. Bell was not hit, but four or five of his men were killed or wounded. He had shot White Wolf several times, and so did others after him; but so tenacious of life was the Apache that, to finish him, a trooper got a great stone and mashed his head.

"This was undoubtedly the greatest duel of modern times; certainly nothing like it ever occurred on the Santa Fe Trail before or since."[33]

Shortly after noon on Sunday, the 23rd of July, we dropped down a grassy slope and into a valley containing some picturesque old buildings, then turned towards the mouth of the canyon and followed an old cutoff up to the Point of Rocks ranch. We were soon greeted by cold beer and the delightful hospitality of Mr. and Mrs. Pete Gaines. The appearance of their somewhat disheveled ranch house, under construction as one of his pet projects, matched that of the rancher-farmer-wrangler-boss who owned and managed the place with the help of one hand: his wife Faye ("born and raised in the county"). Their ranch is beautifully located, if lacking in financial prosperity, and their relationship appeared to be one of the very few fine marriages I have seen. At first, this almost passed me by; I was lost in my observation of his rambling, almost lackadaisical manner, which can easily obscure his fundamental character. Her unsophisticated style, which in an adolescent could be mistaken for giddiness, seemed in an adult charming, youthful and zesty. These traits, combined with the Gaines' willingness to share their interest and knowledge concerning the Trail, almost led me to overlook the more subtle and fascinating fact of their relationship. But as I saw them together, the grace of mutual acceptance, the genuine enjoyment of each other which they displayed, and the unspoken love which seemed to exist between them emanated a comfort which inevitably put us at ease. I came to appreciate this experience in a special way and to regard this couple with an appropriate sense of wonder. Knowing that couples like this existed was both nourishing and reassuring.

As we wandered over the ranch Pete pointed out the old spring, now enclosed, to which a branch of the Trail led travelers who were willing to risk attack from the ever present Indians. There were graves, maintained and protected by him from the parade of treasure hunters who regularly visit with maps, metal detectors, divining rods and instructions from some hallowed document reporting a mine, a stage robbery with buried gold or some other historic Eldorado. He showed us the graves he believes to be the White party, the shaded pools of the spring in the western canyon, and above, rock fortifications on the mesa at the end of an ancient, hand-constructed trail. From the top of the mesa we could see the tipi rings of a camp located near a curious stone wall which stretched out onto the plains for some long forgotten purpose. Back indoors again, we examined documents collected in distant correspondence, including a witness to the possible discovery around the turn of the century of Mrs. White's daughter, now an old woman. But there was no further information about what became of this testimony; it remained a dangling footnote to history. There were pictures—an uncle participating in the gigantic roundups in the last days of the open range after World War I. The cattle would drift into the coolies far to the south to get away from winter storms and in the spring all the ranches in the area would band together for a month of collecting and branding, and then they would herd the cattle back to Springer. There was even a copy of the Springer newspaper containing an item about our ride over the Trail.

Later, camped on top of the mesa, I climbed to the point of the rock just after sunrise to trace the line of the Trail, its passage away to the south marked even now in the cultivated fields by the eroded surface which refuses to yield its historic identity to the digging, cutting erasures of the plough. From behind a bush at my feet a young fawn sprang to follow its cautious, watching mother. Only about two feet tall, it was fat and bushy, and in my surprise I failed to recognize what it was. On the side of the slope grew a gigantic juniper tree some three feet thick and probably much older than the Trail itself. It must have witnessed the straining wagons, marching soldiers, lurking Indians, racing stagecoaches, and agonies of the dying which comprise the story of the old Santa Fe Trail.

Having steered towards this landmark for four days, Sibley and Brown climbed to this same spot on the 18th of October, 1825, where Sibley had one of his more favorable observations of his trip to report:

"While the Men were eating and the Horses grazing, Mr. Brown and I took our rifles and walked onto the Point of Mound, No. 6 at A (on his profile of the landscape) which we reached after a Walk of about 1-1/2 Miles, over level stony Prairie. We ascended to the Top of the Mound, which is probably about 500 feet above the level of the Plain, and staid there an hour, climbing about over the Rocks, of which it seems to be chiefly composed.

"From the top of this height we had a very full view of the great Range of Mountains before us. It appears to be only a few Miles off, tho' in fact it was near 40. Many of the highest points are covered with snow. This view is truly sublime. At the foot of this Mound, or Mountain, are several very large Springs of excellent water. . . ."[34]

Ancient juniper at Point of Rocks

Very soon after this, his party left the main route of the Trail and took the Cimarron Canyon route into Taos, in an effort to "prove" the existence of a wagon route over the mountains. Later when he had returned to Kansas and had almost completed the work on the survey, his camp was struck by lightning:

"At about 5 p.m. during a thunder Storm, a flash of Lightning Struck our Camp. The facts of this incident are as I should conceive Singular. . . . The flash Struck my Tent on one corner, Splintered the upright, passed thro' a leather Iron framed Trunk, which it tore considerably, melted the case of a Pocket Compass in the Trunk (Missing Some Powder) Scorched

Some woolen Socks. It Split the other upright. I was lying asleep on my Pallet on one Side of the Tent, my Feet near the Trunk and my Head near the Pole least damaged. The Shock awoke me to the most painful and alarming Sensations, for my Right Side, which I lay on, was for a Minute bereft of feeling nearly. My foot Seemed Reduced to jelly, having no feeling. A whirring noise passed thro' my ears continually and the Tent was filled with Smoke and Strewed with Splinters. In the other Tent were Six persons; one of whom was Standing against the front Post. He was Struck down and was Senseless for Some time. The top of the Pole Split. One of the others was Severely Shocked, the Rest but Slightly. My own escape was wonderful indeed. Recovered the circulation in my foot and leg in about an hour but am a little deaf and Still having Singing and whirring in my ear."[35]

As we camped upon the mesa high above the prairie for the first time, a bright moon lighting the scene below, we were provided with a new perspective and a beautiful location to think about the last 170 miles of the trip. Because of the arduous detours required to locate grain along the Trail, we decided to leave it at intervals, planning the goals we were to set for each day's riding. Having ridden a distance of 165 miles in 20 days, we now figured to make an average of 24 miles a day for the remaining distance. Actually, our meandering had made it farther than this so we were not being too unrealistic. We dropped grain at stops in Wagon Mound and Fort Union, New Mexico, leaving only one stop without feed, and then left the car outside of Las Vegas. This would be the final 90 miles across the plains until we entered the Pecos canyon country leading into Santa Fe. We had been on the road for three weeks and had come a little less than halfway, although only two weeks of that was actual riding. Now we were planning to double our pace.

The day we left was blazing hot and we prepared ourselves by bathing in the cattle tank while the horses had their final measure of grain for the next 26 hours and 50 miles. It always seemed to take us longer than expected to break camp, and by the time we rode away from the ranch it was noon. Pete came back from ploughing and drove up to wish us godspeed. West we rode, the *Sangre de Cristo* mountains looming before us, even now touched with snow at the crest, and followed the choppy hills and gullies towards Chico Creek, eventually crossing the Canadian. The crossing, *El Vado de Las Piedras*, was the last chance to get across before the rugged, black-walled canyon became too steep and rough. It has been the scene of Indian battles, and the Pawnees used to camp there on their annual raids into Mexico for horses and slaves. Located there was a stage station; which in earlier times marked the frontier where Mexican troops met the wagon trains to escort them to Santa Fe, not so much for their protection as to keep them from repacking wagons and hiding goods to avoid import taxes. Matt Field, young poet, actor, journalist, and rejected suitor escaping west to resolve the dilemma between marriage, ministry, and theater, traveled and wrote about the Trail in the scant five years his fragile health was to afford him. He describes his experience with the Mexican troops who were escorting his party on the return to the Arkansas river in Kansas:

"It was on the fifth day of our travel homeward, after leaving San Miguel, when the mountains were slowly lessening behind us, and far away before us stretched the great plains, that our attention was attracted at about eleven o'clock a.m. by the appearance of some three or four objects in motion at a great distance away to our right. A few indistinct spots appeared which would scarcely have been discernible at all had they not been in motion. We continued on our way with our eyes fixed upon the far horizon where these objects were seen, not apprehending danger, though being in a region much frequented by marauding tribes, we felt probably a sufficient mingling of apprehension to enliven our curiosity. It was soon evident that what we saw could not be buffalo, and a very few moments more brought us to the conviction that a band of wild horses was approaching us, for the swift and graceful lope of that animal became discernible, and as those in advance rose more distinctly into sight other spots appeared behind, and little knots of five or six were seen scattered about the same portion of the prairie, all seemingly moving toward where we were.

"Suddenly one of the Mexican soldiers, who had ridden off to some distance for the purpose of scanning more nearly the advancing objects, was seen to turn and make back toward the caravan, seemingly in great confusion and surprise. When near enough to make himself heard he shouted to us, 'Indios! Indios! Camanches! Camanches!' and instantly the wagons were drawn up forming a *corral,* into which all the loose animals were driven. Lieutenant Hernandez, who commanded our escort of twenty-five soldiers, furnished us by the Governor of Santa Fe, gave us now a specimen of his military capacities, and set about arranging for defence with great coolness and deliberation. Some description of these soldiers is necessary, as also of the condition and strength of our whole party.

"There were five leaders, each of whom employed from five to ten retainers or attendents.—The chief of these leaders is entitled to first attention. He always rode a more than ordinary sized mule, rather tough looking but very docile and very strong. His heavy saddle was ornamented with brass and silver headed nails, driven into the high pummel and back, and forming fanciful and unmeaning devices. The bridle—the wooden stirrups, with their thick and heavy leather guards—the Spanish bit, locking the poor animal's mouth up, and not suffering it to eat or drink, with the jingling ornaments hanging under the jaw—the skins hanging from the pummel, guarding the rider's legs from sun, and rain, and cold,—all these were more or less decorated with knobs and plates of fine silver, but so coarsely worked as to look no better than as many bits of tin. *Don Jose*, upon his mule, was a very formidable looking person, one who was so completely inoffensive. He was master of a very beautiful and very old double-barreled shot gun, and ditto broadsword. These were invariably every morning fastened securely to the pummel of his saddle, and taken off again at night, by a servant; and the writer upon this emergency, finding *Don José* in some perplexity with his weapons, went to his assistance, and found that the shot gun was entirely useless, the nipples being broken and filled with fragments of caps, and the broad sword was so rusted within the scabbard that no effort could extricate it, and it was not actually drawn during the whole course of our travel. Such was *Don Jose* for a warrior, and such, with little variation, may serve as a description of the other Spanish traders and their servants.

"The uniform of the soldiers was as follows:—A round jacket, and pantaloons open on the outside from the knee down, with cuffs, collars, and other trimmings of red flannel; leather leggings tied round the calves and ankles, and coarse shoes. Their weapons were—a short *escopeta* or fusil, a long iron pointed lance, and a knife stuck in the belt. They were all mounted on mules, and each carried, hanging to his saddle, a long rope with a slip noose at one end, and a hollow gourd for transporting water. They were in truth as good a sample of a tattered host of mounted scare crows as were ever dignified with the name of soldiers, yet they manifested little alarm, and having been placed in the best defensive order by the lieutenant, and the brass cannon having been drawn in front of the encampment, ready for action, each man planted his lance in the ground, cocked his fusil, and awaited the approach of the enemy.

"Five of the objects that we had seen were now swiftly approaching us, and the forms of the Indians were distinctly discernible, mounted upon their half wild horses. Other groups were hurrying on behind, numbering in all something less than a hundred, though others were still rising into sight in the distance, and of course we could form no conjecture of how many were yet behind. Our lieutenant was undoubtedly a brave little fellow (a man of slender but sinewy mould, well traced features, deep, dark, flashing eyes, and an eagle nose), and to his spirited conduct on this occasion it is likely we were in a great measure indebted for our subsequent safety. After arranging the camp for the defence, he took the bridle from his mule and placed it in the mouth of a swift horse, and jumping upon its naked back, he dashed off to meet the approaching Indians, ordering no man to follow him unless he should make signal for assistance by firing his *escopeta*.

"In a very short space of time he was at such a distance as made it impossible for us to distinguish his form from those of the Indians, until presently we saw him wheel and ride along in front of the approaching enemy, flourishing his short broadsword above his head, the blade of which glanced in the midday sun, glittering defiance at the red marauder. Here the lieutenant took his stand, and a single Indian advanced to meet him. After spending a few moments in conversation, they advanced side by side toward the camp, and in twenty minutes more the whole scattered band of Camanches, numbering between three and four hundred, had advanced and completely hemmed in our camp, containing about sixty-five souls.

"They were intimidated, however, by the bold and well prepared appearance we made (though indeed much of it was but appearance), but most of all, the sight of the cannon was most effectual in arousing their fears; and as one after another came nearer, to reconnoitre us their eyes were instantly fixed upon the brass field piece. They sat upon their horses with as much carelessness as though they were lounging on buffalo skins within their wigwams. From men of sixty to boys of ten, all seemed equally at home upon horseback, and their whole appearance was no sign of civilization about them;—from head to foot they were Indian—close fitting jackets of deer skin, cut out in small crescents which in a slight degree gave a resemblance of scale armour, long hair flying in the breeze; and not one of them was without a bow in one hand, and a bundle of barbed arrows in the other, while they held their slight yet stronger deer skin bridles in their teeth. Five hundred arrows might have been launched at us there before we could have fired one ball from our cannon, which conveyed such terror to our enemies. But, although of all the Indian tribes the Camanche is most warlike and dangerous to the trader, yet was this party that now crossed our path thoroughly frightened, and Lieutenant Hernandez understood their perplexity well, and knew as well how to profit by his advantage; and he talked to the savages as though they were all at his mercy, and he could, if he pleased, exterminate them all in an instant. They said they were in search of buffalo, and had no intention to molest us, upon which Hernandez told them they might depart, assuming an air as though he had magnanimously granted them their lives. They care little for the Spaniards, but they dread the Americans; and the first question these Indians asked of us was how many Americans were in our party.

"Hernandez, still maintaining his confident demeanor, ordered the camp to be struck, and the Camanches, after hovering around us for two or three hours, at last went off in scattered groups, as they had approached us. They were covered from head to foot with vermilion; and as they dashed along the prairie upon their untamed horses, with their long hair streaming behind them, they seemed like mounted flames of fire, and the very horses seemed to spurn the ground, as though they were under the control of devils!"[36]

As we rode over the steep hills, the Trail had eroded into deep draws, and we followed its rugged progress until we came to a gully full of strange rocks. There were huge concretions with crystals in them and mud shales with shells and mollusks, and we crawled around trying to collect perfect samples of rocks which were too much for us to carry. At one point I led my horse up out of the draw to picket him while I searched the bottom. Climbing up I spooked a coyote which had been sleeping under the bank not 15 feet away. She jumped up and clambered up the bank opposite from me as I grabbed my camera and tried to focus on her, but the lens was too far off, and as I twisted wildly to correct the distance

Canadian River Crossing with wagon ruts, 1935 *(Denver Public Library)*

Kansas flower in July

Author

Author packing

Jack Underhill in Truchas

Jack and Jeanie

Trail into the Springs

The author

The Trail into Wagon Bed Springs

The Cimarron bends: temperature 110 F

Water break at the bends

Crossing the Cimarron quicksands

Author leading the packhorse

Rediscovering the Trail

Middle Springs and Kansas' Point of Rocks

Kansas sunset

A rock outcropping provides a break

With an inscription

The Trail from Willow Bar

Riding into Upper Springs, Oklahoma panhandle

Inscription at Cold Springs

Storm brewing in the No Man's Land

Linda at play with the author

Approaching McNees crossing

Trail erosion

Mt.Clayton and the lava flow

Buffalo wallow and the Sierra Grande

Storm camp

Storm camp at Mt. Clayton

The storm engulfs us

Antelope on the horizon

Point of Rocks, New Mexico

Point of Rocks ranch

Jack and Pete Gaines viewing tipi rings

Pete shows me Allen grave, 1858

The Dorsey mansion

Eliza at the Dorsey mansion

Eroded ruts at Chico Creek

Ruts toward Wagon Mound, first town on the Trail

Ft. Union ruins

Jaffa at Tiptonville stage stop

Stage station corral

Stage station corral

Inside fireplace

Las Vegas, New Mexico plaza

Las Vegas, New Mexico plaza

Kearny Gap, 1972

Pigeons ranch, 1972

Glorieta battlefield and Trail bridge

With Jaffa at Glorieta

First view of Santa Fe

Home again, head for the barn

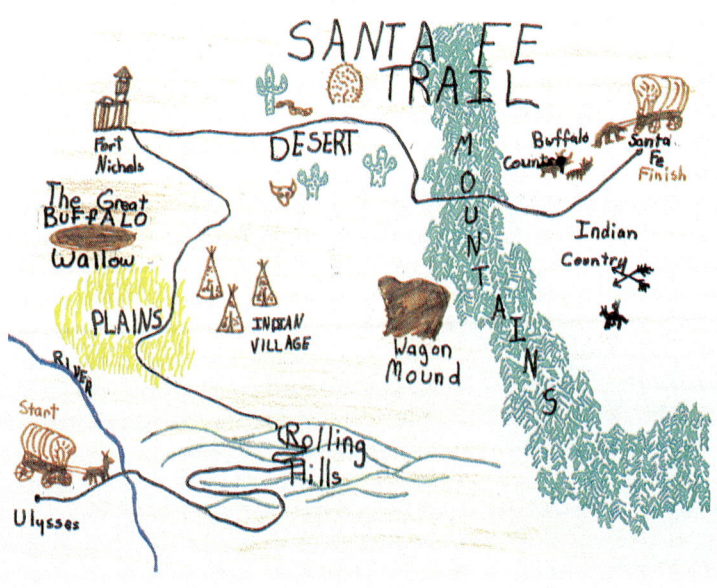

Jaffa map

finder, she disappeared over the hill and out of sight kicking up dust behind her.

We crossed the Chico Creek Ranch, another prosperous looking European style farm with stone buildings and paving stones across the corral, and rode out into open country again for our first view of the Wagon Mound, its bent-looking profile of a prairie schooner a beautiful landmark to the traveler still 40 miles away. Riding up Chico Creek, we reached some cattle pens near the Springer road. Here would be a good place to rest the horses. Dismounting, we watched the summer thunderheads building up miles away towards the mountains. One grew so big that it blotted out the afternoon sun and sent gray sheets of rain sloping to the ground obscuring the land behind it. It was south of us now but moving east, and it was debatable whether its fringes would reach us. We stared at it awhile and then I climbed up onto the loading chute, the highest thing around, to get a better view of its direction. The cloud seemed to be drifting north as it moved and I decided we had better prepare for the storm. As I turned to climb down I heard a sizzling behind me, followed by a crack. Instinctively I crouched down as behind me, not 75 feet away, a cloud of dust rose next to a yucca plant where the bolt had struck. Then lightning broke loose all around us, and the wind shifted, blowing the clouds our way. It was the closest call I'd had, and unnerved me somewhat. We climbed under the boards of the ramp and wrapped the poncho around us as sheets of rain, driven by the strong winds, swept over us, turning the surface of the ground into a flowing torrent and splashing water up under our canvas. Here we waited out the storm, which closed in so thick that we were unable to see more than a few hundred feet, as the horses patiently stood with their tails to the downpour, their heads hung low and the saddles and blankets soaking up the water for our future comfort.

Finally the storm blew over and the next two hours were uneventful, except that as we crossed the highway, a car came honking by at 70 miles an hour, and it was Faye returning from Springer. What timing! That night we camped in an old adobe ruin, for the sky was a crescendo of ominous-looking clouds, flashing sheets of lightning, and occasional sprinkling of rain. The sunset was dazzling as we sat atop the broad grass-covered bluff above the Canadian river. But our water tank contained a murky gray liquid with a sulfurous smell and acidic taste. I thought it was bad and so we climbed up the tower to spin the fan and draw fresh water. In the dark, the blades spun around and chopped into my arm, leaving a deep gash which I did not pay any attention to until morning, when I awoke to find my sleeping bag painted in red. I fashioned a stitch of tape and wrapped it to keep it clean; it is now a permanent addition to my topography.

In spite of my efforts the water came out just as vile as the potion before us and we concluded that this concoction of lime and Alka-Seltzer was the available water supply for the region. I could not stand to drink it even though I was thirsty, and Red never drinks much any way, but Jack and Linda went at it and together shared the fate of its emetic powers for the next 24 hours. And if we thought Trail Chef Stroganoff was bad before when we made it with mineral water, this time it turned out to be criminally vile. So we fortified our meal with a little grain alcohol and orange crystals, garnished with fresh lemon, and blasted our way through dinner.

The next day we crossed the river which figured so prominently in the Trail's annals, and encountered the several branches of the Trail which join at this stretch: the Sibley route to Taos, the Colmor Cutoff to

The only use for water at Taylor Springs

Fort Union, as well as other shortcuts and bypasses. All day we rode towards the beautiful profile of the Wagon Mound, parallel to the mesas and foothills of the *Sangres*. Clusters of showers fell on them by afternoon and the country changed from dry, barren and hot to green savanna, shaded by the summer clouds. The water continued to be mineral and added to the early inhospitability of the land.

Late in the afternoon I encountered a large antelope and was giving him slow chase when three Palominos came prancing into sight. At their appearance the horses broke into a frantic run and we lost control of them. Big Red, who had earlier been dragging himself down the road as though it were his last effort, now became a raging, charging stallion bent upon a display of strength and speed previously unequaled. We were streaking across the prairie with perhaps a mile between us and the small group ahead. No effort on my part would bring him under control as he charged like a demon across the space dividing us. Putting all my weight against his left rein, I gradually diverted him from his race and swung him in an arc about half a mile wide until he calmed down enough to be controlled. Red then began to run towards the horses once more in a more subdued dash. Very soon we were joined by a large antelope buck which raced along beside in a measured pace an even 200 yards off to the left. As we approached the horses Red began to neigh and they responded by dancing and snorting. Behind me Jack's horse reacted with similar excitement and abandon, casting off his baggage as he came running towards us. Sleeping bag, food, and other contents from the pack were bounced off and left in the dusty road.

For the rest of the day the horses were charged up; they usually acted like this only after a day of rest and a good measure of grain. It was a good thing, for the 25 miles we covered that day kept us riding until nine o'clock at night and required our greatest efforts at the very end. About three miles from Wagon Mound we drew within sight of the highway; soon after that the Trail turned west across the railroad and highway to the Santa Clara springs. Here we entered a marsh which looked like no great obstacle until we waded out into its sinking salty expanse. As we entered the mud flats, crisscrossed by channels of slimy water, a hord of mosquitoes arose and settled in a cloud over both man and horse. They were so thick and so unused to human fodder that as they eagerly feasted on my blood, I could wipe a hand down my arm and kill dozens at a pass. As we rode what must have been a mile across the marsh, they swarmed up, penetrating every opening in my clothes, flying into my ears and eyes and mouth, and all the time the high-pitched buzzing, whining, hissing driving me out of my mind as I slapped feverishly at every exposed piece of skin. On we rode and thrashed. Straight ahead were the lights of the station where we had left the grain. Then within several hundred yards of it we hit the fence. No gate. Should we pull it down and get out of this horror show? But neither of us wanted to get off and stand there to do it while the ravenous creatures swarmed over us in the last desperate effort to devour us completely. Anything to keep moving. So we turned back into the swamp and headed east to find a gate and risk the inevitable shivers of yellow fever which would probably climax this disaster. Running, trotting, swimming we found a break in the fence and made it up to a gaping irrigation ditch above. It was almost dark as I tried to urge Red into the ditch to reach the road at the other side. But the wide black water looked to him like a yawning mouth, ready to swallow him in a gulp and he refused to go down the side. Unwilling to reason patiently at this point I spurred him with demands that he get across. Suddenly he coiled up and sprang from the bank like Pegasus, sailing through the air so unexpectedly that he almost left me suspended above the water. I was out of the saddle in the air when I caught the saddle horn with my hand which let me accompany him for the remainder of his flight. It was a vast leap and beautifully executed; we landed safely on the other side.

Jack and I rode into Wagon Mound as the evening finally closed in about us. Dogs ran out to bark at the horses intruding upon their domain and children ran along side us in playful excitement. A car, part of the evening promenade, would cruise down the street, whip a U-turn, and then cruise past in rapping deliberation. The sights and sounds of civilization were upon us. After riding what in direct distance was 215 miles, we had entered our first town. Down the dusty street we saw the glowing sign, "Budweiser," and leaving the horses in custody of the jubilant Spanish boys playing in front of us, we entered to partake of one of the real luxuries of town.

7 ∞ The Path to the Present

Although Wagon Mound was our first town on the Trail, in frontier times it was only a stop at the Santa Clara Spring, the first town actually lying ahead—Las Vegas, founded in 1835, and San Miguel, the original harbinger of civilization to the first travelers.

This location was reputed to be a favorite location of the Indians from which to ambush wagons. Kenyon Riddle tells of the ambush of a stage and the killing of its ten occupants here in 1850. The Indians, Jicarilla Apaches and Utes, then traveled east, where a following detachment of troops found a picture of the massacre drawn by an Indian and left for them near Rabbit Ears. And Inman tells of the New Mexico trader, John L. Hatcher, who outwitted a party of Comanches during a wary encounter beneath the mesa in 1858. As Hatcher's party of 15 wagons approached the Wagon Mound, 300 painted Indians suddenly charged over the hill upon them. After they exchanged the signs of peace, the Indians' headmen were invited to be seated and have some sugar, a customary gift offered by traders when peaceably intercepted by Indians. As he tells it:

"The sweet-toothed warriors helped themselves liberally, and affected much delight at the way they were being treated; but Hatcher, with his knowledge of the savage character, was firm in the belief that they came for no other purpose than to rob the caravan and kill him and his men.

"They were Comanches, and one of the most noted chiefs of the tribe was in command of the band, with some inferior chiefs under him. I think it was Old Wolf, a very old man then, whose raids into Texas had made his name a terror to the Mexicans living on the border.

"While the chiefs were eating their saccharine lunch, Hatcher was losing no time in forming his wagons into a corral, but he told his friends afterward that he had no idea that either he or any of his men would escape; only fifteen or sixteen men against over three hundred merciless savages, and those the worst on the continent, and a small corral,—the chances were totally hopeless! Nothing but a desperate action could avail, and maybe not even that. Hatcher, after the other head men had finished eating, asked the old chief to send his young warriors away over the hill. They were all sitting close to one of the wagons, Old Wolf, in fact, leaning against the wheel resting on his blanket, with Hatcher next to him on his right. Hatcher was so earnest in his appeal to have the young men sent away, that both the venerable villain and his other chiefs rose and were standing. Without a moment's notice or the slightest warning, Hatcher reached with his left hand and grabbed Old Wolf by his scalp-lock, and with his right drew his butcher knife from its scabbard and thrust it at the throat of the chief. All this was done in an instant, as quick as lightning; no one had time to move. The situation was remarkable. The little, wiry man, surround by eight or nine of the most renowned warriors of the dreaded Comanches, stood firm; everybody was breathless; not a word did the savages say. Hatcher then said again to Old Wolf, in the most determined manner: 'Send your young men over the hill at once or I'll kill you right where you are!' holding on to the hair of the savage with his left hand and keeping the knife at his throat.

"The other Indians did not dare to make a move; they knew what kind of a man Hatcher was; they knew he would do as he had said, and that if they attempted a rescue he would kill their favourite chief in a second.

"Old Wolf shook his head defiantly in the negative. Hatcher repeated his order, getting madder all the time: 'Send your young men over the hill, I tell you!' Old Wolf was still stubborn; he shook his head again. Hatcher gave him another chance: 'Send your young men over the hill, I tell you, or I'll scalp you alive as you are!' Again the chief shook his head. Then Hatcher, still holding on the hair of the stubborn victim, commenced an incision in the head of Old Wolf, for the determined man was bound to carry out his threat; but he began very slowly.

"As the chief felt the blood trickle down his forehead, he weakened. He ordered his next in command to send the young men over the hill and out of sight. The order was repeated immediately to the warriors, who were astonished spectators of the strange scene, and they quickly mounted their horses and rode away over the hill as fast as they could thump their animals' sides with their legs, leaving only five or six chiefs with Old Wolf and Hatcher.

"Hatcher held on like grim death to the old chief's hair, and immediately ordered his men to throw the robes out of the wagons as quickly as they could, and get in side themselves. This was promptly obeyed, and when they were all under the cover of the wagon sheets, Hatcher let go of his victim's hair, and, with a last kick, told him and his friends they could leave. They went off and did not return."

And lucky they were after a provocation like that!! It may seem surprising that the Comanches didn't come back and try to "raise the hair" on all of them, but many observers of those times claim Indians were not likely to attack a well-armed and prepared party, because the threat of losses was too great. On the other hand, such an insult was grounds for demotion of a war chief and would hardly be preferable to death.

While our branch of the Trail actually followed the present highway to Watrous, we decided to cross the Turkey Mountains and join the mountain route for the ride into Fort Union. The Fort was a major landmark on the Trail, erected initially as dirt breastworks; its star-shaped trenches are still a visible reminder of the defense against the march of General Henry Sibley's Confederate troops. (Sibley was a nephew to the author and surveyor cited in this book.) Eventually, it became an elaborate military community with streets, shops, a hospital and a thousand troops. Before its closing in 1891 it served as the base for supplies and

Aerial view of Fort Union showing Trail from the Turkey mountains, 1930
(Museum of New Mexico)

military operations in the final wars of subjugation of the Southwestern Indians.

Asking at a local store, we got some rather imprecise directions to the road, one of the many branches of the Trail, which crossed the Turkey Mountains and issued onto the plains above Fort Union. Disregarding the distances, which were a matter of controversy between our informants, I kept track of the number of right and left turns, which seemed to be a matter of greater consensus, and we headed west along Highway 120 to the point where we turned off the road and headed for the pass into the mountains. Multiple sets of ruts indicated various short cuts and stage roads around and through the mountains, and just before entering the rocky pass we stopped to check our directions at a large white stone ranch house. While I picked apples and the horses grazed on the long blades of orchard grass, Jack listened to the man describe the series of lefts and rights which we should follow; as the Trail passed right through here our guide concluded that "we couldn't miss it." I was already saturated with instructions and barely paid any attention to these. We pushed on into the narrow canyon where the stream had cut away the banks, forcing the wagon road into a web of detours which cut up the floor of the valley into numerous gullies. As we passed a recent grave and entered a junction of two canyons, I said, "I think this is where the fellow in town told us to go left." "No, that guy back there just said we keep to the right," Jack answered and he rode on down the more traveled road. That little juncture cost us a day lost in the mountains, but it was hours before we knew we were lost. And as we groped through oak brush and down into watery hollows the country looked less and less like it should according to the directions we were supposedly following.

Crossing the river and riding up the road, we spooked a young cow elk coming down the hill towards us. Some 40 feet away she stopped to look at us with an attitude of surprise, then turned and scampered across the slope above us, stopping once more to assure herself of the necessity of the detour before disappearing from sight. We stopped to lunch in a little glen by a pool of water with large overhanging trees. The sun was hot, the shade was cool and it seemed strange to be beneath these trees with a mountain brook beside us after so many days of unrelieved prairie. Being confined in these close mountains was an alien feeling after having spent weeks riding toward the horizon. At the same time the coolness and green shelter of the trees gave me a sense of intimacy after living in constant exposure.

Riding up onto a small divide we were still headed west instead of south and as we crossed down into a small mountain meadow we could see the plains to the north through the gap. We were riding the full length of the mountains, parallel to the Gallinas route which had led around the mountains and which we decided was the long way. Only we were following it by crossing the mountains instead of following the level plains. Rather than proceed out to Gallinas we took a trail heading off to our left in final hope of reaching some short cut out, but it soon ended in thick woods and steep canyons which were so frightening to the horses that we decided to give up and go back to the road. On the plains again, Gallinas lay to the north of us and we headed west around the spur of the hills where we had spent the day in pointless wandering.

It was late afternoon and Fort Union still lay a dozen miles ahead as we trotted over the grasslands, past various ruins, adobes, and a stage station. We were riding at an altitude of 7,000 feet on the high plains which sloped out of the tree-skirted hills down to the Coyote Creek some four miles to our right. Small herds of antelope grazed around the several water holes and scattered as we pressed our horses forward in a steady trot. One, two, three hours passed until finally the sun hung just above the low ridge on the western side of the valley, and I hurried ahead to a small hill in order to get a few pictures of the Fort in the late afternoon. As we followed the Trail ruts to the Fort, it was dusk and becoming difficult to see. We came to a fence, one of those steel numbers with innumerable spacers and no gate so we stepped it down and rode over. The mud and brick spires of the Fort's ruined walls and chimneys were silhouetted like dead trees against the afterlight. The ruts passed the south side and crossed the road, heading towards the houses of the park employees where we had left the grain.

As I rode across a field and between two houses, some kids were in front playing basketball with a young park official who looked more like a camp counselor than a park authority. We asked for the superintendent (we'll call him Señor Ramírez) whom I had met previously and at whose house I had left the horses' grain. When informed that he wasn't there now, we asked this fellow if he could sell us some bread and milk for our supper, but he didn't have any. It was dark, we were tired after our long ride, I was less than interested in listening to him when he asked us where we had come from today and then began to inform us of all the regulations we had broken by not driving in by car, unarmed, horses crated and deodorized. His bossy self importance was deeply offensive. He informed us where we couldn't sleep, where we couldn't leave the horses, and what we couldn't do while we were there until we decided that one of the things that we weren't going to do was listen to this boy scout preach at us. So we headed for the Ramirez house, guided by several of his kids, where we fed and watered the horses and drank Kool Aid to wash the unpleasant taste out of our mouths.

The superintendent was Chicano and his household was one of those delightful Spanish homes, so typical of New Mexico, full of warmth and acceptance and genuine regard for each other, especially noticeable among the children. I wondered how it was possible for a Chicano to rise in the Federal bureaucracy and not become the cultureless, characterless, insecure gelding which most social organizations require of people without white Anglo bourgoise backgrounds. People usually seem to give in to the required model: defensive, timid of showing any identity which doesn't fit the bland but manipulative stereotype, or gleeful wielders of

Mechanics corral, 1866 *(Museum of New Mexico)*

Officers Row, 1884 *(Museum of New Mexico)*

mildly sadistic powers, which spills over into the family. Here was a family of delightful people: warm and open, capable of feeling and expression, genuine in their concern for each other and a complete surprise in the context of civil servants and executive offices. From the inferences about family history, I gathered that this career had been a checkered success, but I was impressed that traditional identity had survived at all. In this enchanting setting we bathed for the first time since Seneca, and ate in the darkness created by electrical blackout, surrounded by children and domestic conversation. Then picketing the horses for the night, we returned to the sticky weeds within sight of the skeletal ruins.

The next morning we were up at sunrise, taking pictures. The old stone jail, with its vaulted doors and ringing echoes, had held Geronimo and Billy the Kid. The mechanics' corral, with its odd wooden arch and hatched floor pattern, contrasted strangely to the old photos showing wagons, cavalrymen and crisp colonial architecture. While I took my equipment back to the horses and got some breakfast, Jack went to park headquarters to appease the "savage blow of nature" and had a cordial meeting with the superintendent. When he returned we packed up our equipment and loaded the horses so we could depart after our more thorough tour of the ruins. We returned to the headquarters and I looked forward to seeing Sr. Ramirez again, but when we rode up boyscout had apparently huddled with the super and the boss was now a *changed* man. He insisted our horses were dangerous and should be picketed where they could not damage the near-empty parking lot. And he watched over us in nervous disapproval as I dismantled the .22 rifle in my scabbard. Finally, he wanted to know why we had "destroyed" the fence coming in (he wasn't interested in "why") and did we know that we were destroying property of the U.S. Government. (I had mistakenly assumed that the parks belonged to the people of the United States. How naive!) All this dampened our interest in seeing the Fort and my enthusiasm for visiting with Sr. Ramírez, so after a confused performance of a couple of items of business and a quick look around the museum we left what was the most squalid

Water drain

Mechanics corral, 1972

Today's walls

Mechanics corral, 1972

experience of the whole trip. We were totally bummed out. In a rather frightening way I had discovered the answer to my query about minorities and the Federal bureaucracy. This has to be the ultimate in diabolical, totalitarian cultural imperialism. Now we really felt like we were back in civilization again and it was such a horrifying specter.

From that experience we had nowhere to go but up, but we were to go up mighty slowly. On through the Tiptonville stage stop, our entry into Watrous (called then La Junta for the junction of the Mora and Sapello rivers) was exciting because the road was lined with overhanging trees which touched at the crown and gave one the feeling of shelter and grace

Santa Fe Trail into Tiptonville

one gets from an old country road. As one enters town, the trees strike a note of comfort and welcome, like a resting place at the end of the trail. Here the Cimarron and mountain routes rejoined and many of the old buildings had the appearance of historical Trail days about them. Aside from that, however, the historical look was almost completely obliterated by modern times. Beginning at this juncture and with the exception of a few places on the Pecos and outside of Santa Fe, the road succumbs to the racing scream of the super highway, and the disapprobation of jealous property owners.

From Watrous to Las Vegas is 18 miles of rush and noise and human indifference. Beautiful grasslands by car, the highway passes smooth and fast through the slightly undulating meadow. It has always seemed somehow a dramatic contrast to its natural undeveloped setting. By horse, this becomes an inhospitable and violated land. The Trail crisscrosses the interstate with its fences lacking gates. Iron cattle guards and precarious concrete bridges make it impossible to follow the shifting curls of the ruts forcing a choice of one side, outside the road, or the sloping right of way beside the highway. We chose the highway and what a disaster it was.

Ox train on Railroad avenue, Las Vegas, New Mexico, 1910 *(Denver Public Library)*

The disrupted ecology has left the soil rotten, the vegetation spotty. Varmints have tunneled into the gravel leaving mounds and holes, and coarse weeds blocked our access in thick, prickly clumps. Even without the broken bottles, cardboard boxes, cans, plastic, wood, paper, wire, steel, carcasses, cups, and tires the going was unpleasant. But the speeding train, due in Albuquerque and running behind schedule with its windows where no one saw, its passing cars containing dull, blank looks on strange faces, provided an experience with travelers totally different from what we had seen on other roads. At a rest stop Jack led his horse up to a trailer and asked the lady for a drink of water; but she didn't have any to spare before she sped off on the 10-minute drive to Las Vegas. The endless heat, the constant noise, hazardous footing, and monotonous highway turned the tedious distance into a depressing nightmare. By afternoon we were more than ready to take one of the rare crossroads leading off the highway and follow the old highway towards town. Within sight of the tracks we followed old Highway 85 until we came to a shaded homestead just across the creek.

"Do you have a place where we could pasture our horses for a day or so?"

"Why yes, in that field just across the road and down a half mile, and there's a stream, and a bunk house where you can stay."

It was getting ready to rain as we entered the fence and led the horses through the tall grass to the little two-roomed white house where we unloaded and stashed our stuff.

We had left the car at a gas station north of town and as we crossed the stream and climbed the hill on the other side we saw the sign flashing just across the highway before us. Incredible luck! On the windshield was a note that a friend was coming in from Colorado that night by bus at two in the morning. I called an old buddy who worked at the university and soon we had a comfortable and dry place to bunk down for a couple of days.

The two days spent at Las Vegas ("the meadows") were like none of our other stops thus far. Never had we been so close to a town of any size, nor the amenities and bustle that go with it. My friend's arrival Saturday morning and our stay at Gabino's house added a note of reunion

Old Town, Las Vegas, 1880 *(Denver Public Library)*

Old Town, Las Vegas Plaza, 1882 *(Denver Public Library)*

Plaza in 1882 *(Denver Public Library)*

with ordinary life which presaged our final arrival. There was beer, music, and conversation extending beyond history and survival which had become the major boundaries of our experience. I had made arrangements to pick up one of my daughters for the last few days' journey into Santa Fe. I had wanted them to share in the experience somehow, but she was the only one old enough or sufficiently interested in the adventure to join us. She was to meet us outside of Las Vegas at Tecolote on Sunday afternoon, so we hunted around to find a horse we could use for the last 70 miles. We called various people we knew, advertised on the radio, even checked the local livestock auction but were unable to come up with a thing. So on Sunday afternoon, July 30th, we returned empty handed to our pasture north of town to resume the ride. Approaching town from the north, as all travelers of the Trail had done, afforded none of the bucolic appearance which had characterized the scene in the past.

Susan Magoffin and W. H. Emory, both associated with Kearny's advancing American army in 1846, have left accounts of their experience. Lieutenant Emory, making a military reconnaissance, offers botanical, astronomical, and geographical observations as well; he was witness to the General's proclamation of occupation from the roof of a building on the old plaza. Entering the town on August 14th, Emory gave the following description:

> "As we emerged from the hills into the valley of the Vegas, our eyes were greeted for the first time with waving corn. The stream was flooded, and the little drains by which the fields were irrigated, full to the brim. The dry soil seemed to drink it in with the avidity of our thirsty horses. The village, at a short distance, looked like an extensive brick-kiln. On approaching, its outline presented a square with some arrangements for defense. Into this square the inhabitants are sometimes compelled to retreat, with all their stock, to avoid the attacks of the Eutaws (Utes) and Navajoes, who pounce upon them and carry off their women, children, and cattle. Only a few days since, they made a descent on the town and carried off 120 sheep and other stock. As Captain Cooke passed through the town some ten days since, a murder had just been committed on these helpless people. Our camp extended for a mile down the valley; on one side was the stream, on the other the corn fields, with no fence or hedge interposing. What a tantalizing prospect for our hungry and jaded nags; the water was free, but a chain of sentinels was posted to protect the corn, and strict orders given that it should not be disturbed...."[37]

The town has long since spilled out of the valley and has bypassed the old plaza which was the hub of residence and commerce. As traffic streamed passed we abandoned the highway in favor of the shaded side streets leading to the plaza. We rode into the tree-filled plaza which had been the scene of the first major American proclamation of sovereignty that August 15th, a century and a quarter ago. It had been surrounded by one-story adobe houses then, but now bore the an appearance of the subsequent American rule. Largely Victorian, it was a collection of two-story brick buildings, cornices, sculptured iron work and wooden pillars. Built and then forsaken by American prosperity, it retains the mark of the period two generations after Kearny announced:

"Mr. Alcalde (mayor), and people of New Mexico: I have come amongst you by orders of my government, to take possession of your country, and extend over it the laws of the United States. We consider it, and have done so for some time, a part of the territory of the United States. We come amongst you as friends—not as enemies; as protectors—not as conquerors. We come among you for your benefit—not for your injury.

"Henceforth I absolve you from all allegiance to the Mexican government, and from all obedience to General Armijo. He is no longer your governor (great sensation). I am your governor. I shall not expect you to take up arms and follow me, to fight your own people, who may oppose me; but I now tell you, that those who remain peaceably at home, attending to their crops and their herds, shall be protected by me, in their property, their persons, and their religion; and not a pepper, not an onion, shall be disturbed or taken by my troops, without pay, or by the consent of the owner. But listen! he who promises to be quiet, and is found in arms against me, I will hang!

"From the Mexican government you have never received protection. The Apaches and the Navajoes come down from the mountains and carry off your sheep, and even your women, whenever they please. My government will correct all this. It will keep off the Indians, protect you in your persons and property; and, I repeat again, will protect you in your religion. I know you are all great Catholics; that some of your priests have told you all sorts of stories—that we should ill-treat your women, and brand them on the cheek as you do your mules on the hip. It is all false. My government respects your religion as much as the Protestant religion, and allows each man to worship his Creator as his heart tells him is best. Its laws protect the Catholic as well as the Protestant; the weak as well as the strong; the poor as well as the rich. I am not a Catholic myself—I was not brought up in that faith; but, at least one-third of my army are Catholics, and I respect a good Catholic as much as a good Protestant.

"There goes my army—you see but a small portion of it; there are many more behind—resistance is useless.

"Mr. Alcalde, and you two captains of militia, the laws of my country require that all men who hold office under it shall take the oath of allegiance. I do not wish, for the present, until affairs become more settled, to disturb your form of government. If you are prepared to take oaths of allegiance, I shall continue you in office, and support your authority."

As Emory states, it was a "bitter pill" and during the oath taking the general had to remind the captain of the conquered militia to "look me in the face" as he swore obedience. The Americans had their nerve, for they still had not met the Mexican army in battle, and the 1600-man "Army of the West" faced Governor Armijo's 4,000 men lodged at Apache Canyon to the west. But possibly General Kearny already knew that his $50,000 bribe offered to the governor by trader James Magoffin (Susan's brother-in-law) had had the desired effect, and Armijo was already preparing to flee to old Mexico.

South and west of the plaza, the old section contained adobe houses with a feeling of history about them. Broken plaster revealed thick walls of mud brick. A four sided building with rooms around a common courtyard, and with an arched entryway closed off by a huge wooden door, recalled the old defensive architecture of the seventeenth and eighteenth centuries. Today there are windows cut in the outside walls, but in those days the threat of Indians forced all social intercourse into the protected plaza of the house. Now there were people sitting out on porches in the summer afternoon, exchanging smiles and greetings, or shy laughter with the passing strangers mounted on horseback.

Out of town the excavation of a new four-lane highway competes with the fading furrows of the old Trail for the merging access to the narrow canyon at Kearny Gap. Trees are dwarfed or buried, like the Trail itself, as civilization marches over the signs of the past and witnesses the abandonment of stone barns, corrals, and red adobe buildings. We were in the rolling foothills of the Pecos River *cañon*.

In the late afternoon we rendezvoused at Tecolote and planned to set up camp in the junipers above the town. The town where the Russells established a store in 1866 after leaving Fort Nichols and subsequently retiring from the military looked squalid in its crude stone architecture and belied its size and historic importance on the Trail. Southeast of the plaza a Trail marker stood beside the road where it fords the Pecos River. The plaza had lost its central importance now. A church, abandoned buildings, and a large overhanging cottonwood tree provided signs of its communal past. But there were no stores or commerce beyond children on bicycles and an old man reeling drunkenly from the back of a lathered horse whose mouth was sudsy with cranberry-colored foam where the *borrachón* had hung onto the bit to steady himself and keep from pitching into the dust. Behind him, his nephew followed silently, looking at the strangers collected on horses and cars, watching. Across the footbridge over the river, a group of children raced their small horses into town, making a thundering clatter which caused Red to twist nervously. They passed by, going up the road which climbs the barren hillside where most of Tecolote sprawls on rocky red dust shelves. The lack of trees and green vegetation gave the scene a sense of desolation which seemed to overshadow human occupation but the warm, red New Mexican sun on russet stone walls softened the scene's poverty, at least to the eye.

That night our camp included visitors and we collected juniper

Trail through Kearny Gap (19th century) *(Denver Public Library)*

wood and set up saddles to provide a lounge around the fire. Vicki had brought a birthday cake because that day Jack was thirty-five.

Just before dusk a horseman rode into camp. It was the son of Garza, the man who owns this land, and he was trying to find out who left the gate open. We assure him that we found it open and were discussing things when a pickup truck with an old man, women, and some young kids drove up. It was old Garza with what must have been his third family for his adult children lived in houses scattered around the plaza. We struggled at conversation in heavily accented Spanish and colloquial vocabulary: the Trail was beside the abandoned highway on the hillside below, and, yes, he had some horses we could rent if he could only catch them. So we offered to help him locate them in the morning and made plans to get together at sunrise. But next morning we got up, ate, packed, and still no Garza. Around mid-morning his boy rode up and said they had been trying to catch the horses all morning, but had been unable to find them. Bad enough, I thought, but then the boy said his father wanted eight dollars for our camping on his land. "Eight bucks? For what?" It looked like highway robbery to me. But he said the old man had told us in our parley the night before that he'd come back and collect for using his land. Man, I didn't realize how much we had lost in translation. I asked Jack about it since he'd done most of the talking and interpreting, but it was news to him; and meanwhile, young Garza was standing around waiting to be paid. I was really feeling compromised and the kid was in a difficult position; he didn't like it any more than I did and said if it was up to him we could have stayed for free, but he was on a mission for his father. We stood around in angry irresolution for a minute and had a hasty conference to decide what to do. We were packed up and could be out of there in a matter of minutes: it wouldn't have been hard to tell him to shove it. On the other hand he did own the land, and I was not interested in leaving a string of hostile natives behind, especially after everyone else had been so hospitable. So I told him that eight dollars was too much and offered him four, which he agreed was reasonable, and he took it and left, as anxious to be out of this embarrassment as we were to be rid of him.

We spent most of the day riding toward San Miguel and checking with local people for an extra horse which might make it the last 50 miles into Santa Fe. Vicki and Jaffa spent the day racing each other on horseback, while Jack and I pursued endless empty leads and malicious "helpful" suggestions. By afternoon we had covered half the distance back to Kansas, and we stopped at a cafe and bar near Bernal. The many dark references to the character of the natives made by those travelers of a century ago were beginning to seem more and more *apropos*. Here we encountered the ultimate in useful advice. The horses were tied outside and while a gaggle of young aficionados ogled the beasts, we entered with our improbable party of four. Knowing better than to open a serious conversation with anyone in a bar, we began talking about horses with the afternoon revelers. Outside again we had soon collected a small gang of Chicano men who stood around poking and prodding the horses, exchanging alternately menacing and covetous looks towards the animals and girls, and proffering pledges of aid and useful advice.

One especially valuable piece of information came from a fast talking hombre of about 30, dressed in work clothes and a cap with the word "Cat" above the visor. He circled around the horses making comments about their age, intelligence and musculature, and then, looking at Red with the critical eye of a veteran auctioneer he commented, "This horse will never make it to Santa Fe." NEVER MAKE IT TO SANTA FE! When informed that Red had already made it from Kansas, he reeled a little bit but recovered with the obvious conclusion that we were full of it. He then proceeded to make a very generous offer to buy him. Finally, convinced that Red wasn't for sale, he offered to trade the pair for a couple of horses he guaranteed would get us to Santa Fe. One of the gang owned a string of horses in a nearby town where he lived. (His buddy had informed us with some solemnity that Carlos here, who bore the name of the town, was descended from the family which founded it two centuries before.) And "descended" was the proper term to use, too, for he was carrying on his own version of the family tradition. When we met him he was too drunk to think and the side of his head bore teethmarks where someone had bitten his ear clean off at the skull. It looked like he might have what we needed, however, until it turned out that his price for two days' use was just about what his buddy had offered to pay for my horse. It was becoming obvious that the people of the valley were going to be impossible to deal with, so we decided to move onto a camp in the mesas above San Miguel Crossing and forget trying to get an extra horse: we would just ride double.

8 ∞ Rio Pecos

The canyon of the Pecos River marks the long, rough stretch climbing up to the hills behind Santa Fe. The traveler enters the rolling country west of Las Vegas at an altitude of 6,400 feet, passes Starvation Peak and rides upward through the spotty *piñon* and juniper trees until he reaches the Glorieta Pass at 7,400 feet. Steep ridges and cliffs tower on both the north and south sides and ahead the snowy crags of Pecos and Santa Fe Baldy and the Truchas Peaks reach up to 13,000 feet. All the travelers converge for this section of the Trail and it was here that Gregg

Pecos River Crossing at San Miguel, the former frontier

became apprehensive as he wandered for what seemed an inordinate time after following local instructions:

> "On the following day about the hours of twelve, as I was pursuing a horse path along the course of the Rio Pecos, near the frontier settlements, I met with a shepherd, of whom I anxiously inquired the distance to San Miguel. 'O, it is just there,' responded the man of sheep. 'Don't you see that point of mesa yonder? It is just beyond that.' This welcome information cheered me greatly; for owing to the extraordinary transparency of the atmosphere, it appeared to me that the distance could not exceed two or three miles. 'Está cerquita,' explained the shepherd as I rode off, *'ahora está v. allá'*—'it is close by; you will soon be there.'
>
> "I set off at as lively a pace as my jaded steed could carry me, confident of taking dinner in San Miguel. Every ridge I turned I thought must be the last, and thus I jogged on, hoping and anticipating my future comforts till the shades of evening began to appear, when I descended into the valley of the Pecos, which although narrow is exceedingly fertile and beautifully lined with verdant fields, among which stood a great variety of mud cabins. About eight o'clock I called at one of these cottages and again inquired the distance to San Miguel; when a swarthy-looking ranchero once more saluted mine ears with *'Está cerquita; ahora está v. allá.'* Although the distance was designated in precisely the same words used by the shepherd eight hours before, I had the consolation at least of believing that I was something nearer. After spurring on for a couple of miles over a rugged road, I at last reached the long-sought village."[38]

San Miguel del Vado, 1846 *(Denver Public Library)*

San Miguel del Vado, (early 20th century?) *(Denver Public Library)*

San Miguel, 1972

San Miguel contained the ford of the Pecos River (hence the name *San Miguel del Vado*—of the ford) and was a major stop on the Trail, having numbered 3000 inhabitants at one time against the five dozen of today; it was the oldest of the towns east of Santa Fe and west of the U.S. border. In 1841 President Lamar of Texas sent the disastrous Texas-Santa Fe expedition to assure "union and identity" between his country and the New Mexicans by extending the border of Texas to the banks of the Rio Grande. Governor Armijo's soldiers riding out from Santa Fe over the Trail, intercepted the expedition which had already been overwhelmed by its journey across the Llano Estacado, and held groups of prisoners in jail at the plaza of San Miguel.

Two of the prisoners were executed in the plaza before the eyes of their horrified companions and the rest were marched to prisons in El Paso and Chihuahua, stragglers in the journey being shot and their ears cut off as proof for Armijo that they had not escaped. Two years later another party of Texans sacked the town of Mora to the north and President Santa Ana of Mexico closed the Trail to commercial traffic. But in 1846 the tides of possession shifted and General Kearny moving west from Las Vegas repeated his speech of occupation to the officials of San Miguel and at night camped on the Trail near the town. That night, as the army awaited news of Armijo's opposing forces in the canyon, a soldier described their bivouac:

> "Our camp is around the base of a hill, which is prairie half way up, the other portion being a pretty grove of pines and cedars. A picket guard from the infantry was ordered to be posted on its summit, and I, as officer of the day, went up after night to examine the ground and attend to it. There I had a most lovely sight, the campfires extending in the shape of a half moon around its base at least a mile and a half, the whole army reposing in perfect security, and the busy hum of voices coming up as if from a crowded city."[39]

Some days later the party in which Susan Magoffin was traveling also reached the village and she offered the following observation:

> "... as usual the villagers collected to see the curiosity, and I did think the Mexicans were as void of refinement, judgment, etc., as the dumb animals till I heard one of them say 'bonita muchachita' (pretty little girl). And now I have reason and certainly a good one for changing

Church at San Miguel, 1972

my opinion; they are certainly a very *quick and intelligent people*. Many of the *mujeres* came to the carriage shook hands and talked with me. One of them brought some tortillas, new goat's milk and stewed kid's meat with onions, and I found it much more palatable than 'the dinner at the Vegas.' They are decidedly polite, easy in their manners, perfectly free &c.

"The village of San Miguel is both larger and cleaner than any we have passed: it has a church, and public square, neither of which are in the others."[40]

Some half dozen years before, Matt Field visited the town and attended services in the church, which had originally been built as a mission to the Christianized Indians living there. His impression is more equivocal:

"Doubtless in that old church there were hearts as purely devoted to God as could be found in the cushioned pews of our own splendid tabernacles; for virtue is a thing that falleth as 'the gentle rain from heaven' as well upon the rudest as the most cultivated spot of earth; and though we are prone to place crime with poverty and ignorance, yet we know that the evil which sullies the polish of refinement is as hideous among uncultured men. Yet though pure religion may have existed in that motley congregation, it was an offensive libel on sacred things the manner in which the ceremonies were conducted.

"There were no seats of any kind in the church, and the worshippers were all either standing or kneeling. The mud walls were whitewashed, and a few wretched daubs of paintings, actually frightful to look at, were fastened up, some to rude frames, others hanging in rags with no frames at all. Among these was one piece of rotten canvas, with a little paint still lingering in it, but so completely demolished by time that it was impossible to discover what could have been the subject or design of the artist. It was probably some Madonna or saint, brought from Spain long enough ago to have passed through the wars. In a recess at one side of the alter, stood two men, one playing a fiddle and the other a guitar, and on these instruments the musicians seemed to be studying what kind of an extravagant and fantastic discord they could make. The noise made by two quarrelsome cats was quite as much like music. These musicians composed not only the church choir but also the ball room orchestra, and it may be supposed that they felt a necessity of making as broad a distinction as possible between the dancing and the sacred music.

"In a few moments a priest appeared from an apartment at one side of the altar, and with great precipitation commenced his duties; he went about his sacred functions as though something of much more importance was awaiting his attention, and he had very little time to waste in performing the ceremonies of the mass. After bending one of his knees at the altar, he descended the steps, with a long brush like a musquito flapper in his hand, followed by a lank, uncombed figure, in a long, black gown, bearing a large bowl of holy water. He kicked open a door in the wooden railing of the altar, and advanced among the people, who opened an aisle for him to pass, and dipping sacred fluid he sprinkled the congregation, flirting his brush about and muttering blessings, much more like an angry housewife, hurrying about and scolding servants, than a man of God. This operation performed, he returned to the altar, and contrived to get through the whole mass in about half an hour, and in fifteen minutes after the writer found him smoking a *chupar* in the shop of the only American trader in town. . . .

"A beautiful crystal stream rushes through this town, at no part more than four feet in depth, and so clear that the white pebbles can be seen glittering at the bottom and skipping along with the force of the current. Here in the afternoon, when the heat of the day had passed, groups of girls and children were seen plunging their bare feet into the refreshing stream, and arousing echo with screams of laughter and delight. The writer joined one of these groups, at once to partake of the same luxury and to observe more closely the bathers. Sociably following the old principle of 'when in Rome,' &c. he pulled off his stockings and prairie 'sandal shoon' and sat down with his feet in the water, experiencing a refreshment so delightful that he longed to imitate the happy children, and laugh and shout aloud. But he was alone, and a stranger in a wild and strange place, and happiness only finds voice when kindred voices are near to yield the responsive echo. The children eyed the stranger curiously, and some remarks that were capital food for vanity, fell from the lips of the elder girls concerning the young American; 'el blanco Americano,' whose white feet excited the undisguised admiration of the young ladies. This might have been some gratification to the American had the young ladies themselves thought proper to wash their faces as well as their feet, and get rid of the dirt and red paint which sadly interfered with the effect of bright eyes, round cheeks, and the whitest and most regular teeth in the world. The simple *señoritas* are very fond of vermilion, and they daub it on forehead and nose as well as on the cheeks, showing that their ideas of beauty are in some measure derived from the Indians.

"It is provoking to see really pleasant featured girls so disfigure themselves, and the only bit of gallantry an American would think of offering them would be to dip their heads in the river or dash a bucket of water in their bedaubed faces."[41]

The sun that day had been broiling hot again, and in the afternoon as we rode up into the rough mesas two or three miles from town the heat reflected off the rust-colored sand which was hardened into the desert road beneath us. After setting up our camp and resting in the shade we doubled up on the unsaddled horses and rode back down to the river for a bath. As we crossed the parched fields of sand and clay, mosquitoes would swarm up around our bodies, until great welts appeared on our backs and limbs and their festering itching promised to more than compensate for any comfort gained from refreshing in the river. The thick Russian thistle covered the ground where multiple gullies remained to identify the place where the Trail crossed the river and then continued north towards the nearby town of San José.

As we returned towards camp, hurrying our horses across a stubble field and back to the road where the mosquitoes would finally abandon their feast upon our flesh, the sky was beginning to darken with billowing storm clouds and a gradual crescendo of rumbling thunder accented our splendid setting for the night. Located on the edges of a rocky cliff which sloped down to the flood plain and provided a short but sharp accent for the little road which led up through the large junipers to our concealed encampment, we could see all surrounding countryside and activity and yet remain aloof and detached from its traffic. Behind and to the side, a line of jagged hills and mesas faced out across the valley plain. Below us, a mile away, ran the Trail crossing the Pecos from a long abandoned spur out of Ribera and losing itself in the eroded, weed-covered flats to the west; replaced now, a century later, by the commerce of the railroad within a few feet of the actual route.

I surveyed it from our shelter which for the first time seemed to give me the perspective of historical distance which I had lacked before this camp. It all seemed obsolete now, belonging to another era, long before the present trains which seldom run, and the indistinct town which has faded into obscurity, its plaza gone, its old buildings closed or melting away. And I began to think ahead, of arrival, of greeting, of future plans and consequences, and the distance ahead began to seem more of an obstacle, the slow pace produced impatience. Any crisis now would lose its meaning in a scheme suddenly larger and beyond the simple life which

Approaching San José on the Pecos

now consumed so much attention. And while I did not long to be finished, a different meaning and perspective was growing up inside. There would he no cries of "*carros*," "*Los Americanos*," money or festivities, and we would melt back into an alien way for which the present held no meaning. Only the quiet satisfaction of knowing what we'd done, the learning, and the measure of ourselves. All that really mattered, and yet the passage would be awkward. For riding alone across the land still gives a place to man if only by his minor scale in such a scheme of beauty.

A vision of crowds of people each pursuing their scattered business no matter how important, seemed to breed a deeper sense of obscurity, as if civilized deeds which daily catch us up can really have no meaning. What would it be like to once again do things which now seemed so remote. The ease and comfort, the speed, the overwhelming flow of people, the concerns which would reoccupy me until I overlook and forget the kinds of experience I had here. I risked the awareness of myself, my body, of day and sun and light, of simple efforts and direct rewards, dependence on an animal I learned to understand, and of time which came to mean an angle of the sun and uniform succession to one's feelings; always there,

Entering the town

always regular, never racing by so fast I lose the moment and forget what happens. This place meant never waking up to find myself involved in something I didn't choose or earn. Here I didn't lose sight of things before my eyes because the things inside my head had captured my attention. And when I returned, where would all this go? It seemed so clear right then, but reality would change with other ways and different circumstances.

It was hot again the following day as we followed the worn Trail over the uneven landscape among the *piñon* and juniper trees of the arid countryside. Occasionally, a horse would run over from a long abandoned ranch, red stone buildings forming a desolate but organic unity with the rocky canyon in which it was set, equine curiosity a sharp contrast to the fleeting escape of a timid coyote surprised while on his mealtime rounds. Around noon we reached the town of San José lying over a whitewashed hillside. It reminded me of one of the desolate villages in the impoverished countryside of Spain. We entered a quiet corner of the town, the narrow street distinct between thick walled mud houses and wooden barns placed in corrals bristling with untrimmed posts and shaggy juniper poles.

Jack rides into the plaza

Turning down the lane toward the plaza, an explosion shattered the lazy feeling of hot afternoon and children scurried down the alleys out of sight of the incoming strangers.

Suddenly we found ourselves in a large, open courtyard surrounded by 200 years of architecture and decay. What had once been the highway which entered from the northwest corner tracing a rough paved path around the southern side of the plaza exited at the opposite corner where it dissolved into hayfields and an abandoned bridge across the Pecos. In the center stood the church looking as modern and out of place as such a renovated plaster mission can be in an otherwise historic setting of this type. But for this, the town preserved more of the feeling of the days of the Trail than more important places such as San Miguel and Las Vegas.

We stopped to rest our horses and drink and eat in one of the stores on the plaza. There we asked the storekeeper something of the local history about which the natives seldom seem to have an interest. After a rest in the shade amid old cash registers and oak counters we returned to the nearby highway. The rest of the day would find us near the

San José plaza

super highway struggling with access roads having no gates around their cattle guards or riding the right-of-way and torturing our horses on the bruising gravels along the roadway's path. The towns would all lack flavor and the predominance of the interstate or railroad right-of-way had largely destroyed the country's historic character. Places were gone or changed, like Kozlowski's ranch where Inman reminisced about the passing of the Trail back in the 1880s while sampling the last of their widely-hailed cuisine and matching its decline against the progress of the railroad. Johnson's stage station built in the mid-1800s as a Spanish homestead was Confederate headquarters during the battle of Glorieta in March 1862. A detachment of Colorado volunteers outflanked the Southern army and burned the ammunition and supply train quartered at the station forcing a strategic retreat of the Texas volunteers. Part of the corrals and well remain but the interstate took out the old house a few years ago.

Pockets of history survive; Pigeon's Ranch, field headquarters for the Union forces protecting Fort Union, was the scene of fighting on the second day of the battle of Apache Canyon. Two juniper trees across from the old adobe building bear holes where someone dug out the musket balls

The Church

buried there during the action. The large corrals have melted away and the house is in a shambles, faded contrast to the old days as it crowds against the black top now covering the Trail. The ancient village of Pecos, once the largest of New Mexican pueblos, is said to have contained 2,500 people within its two, four-story communal dwellings. Occupied at the time of Coronado's visit in 1540, it was repeatedly raided by Comanches and swept by disease until by 1838 its 17 survivors abandoned the city to take up residence with the people of Jemez Pueblo. The ancient church attracted exploration by travelers of the Trail. Susan Magoffin stopped there and commented on its appearance in 1846:

"We got off our horses at the door and went in, and I was truly awed. I should think it was sixty feet by thirty. As is the custom among the present inhabitants of Mexico, this pueblo is built of unburnt bricks and stones. The ceiling is very high and doleful in appearance; the sleepers are carved in hiroglyphical figures, as is also the great door, altar and indeed all the little woodwork about it, showing that if they were uncivilized or half-civilized as we generally believe them, they had at least an idea of grandure. Some parts of it, too, have the appearance of turned work, though it is difficult to decide, it is so much battered to pieces. From the church leads several doors, into private apartments of the priests, confession-room, penance chambers, etc.

"One of them only has a fireplace in it, and this is exceedingly small. All around the church at different distances are ruins; the side of one house remains perfect still, and 'tis plain to see a three storied building once was there. The upper rooms were entered by ladder from the outside—and in case of an enemy's coming these ladders were drawn up, and no communication being afforded below they were perfectly secure to cast stones or any other missil at their not so well protected enemy.

"*Mi alma* pointed out to me the door of a room in which he had once slept all night in some of his trips across the plains, and while some of the inhabitants still remained. It was in the second story of a house, which is now fallen in, and the doors so entirely closed by the rubbish (except this room) that it had nothing of the appearance of having been a house.

"The place too has the appearance of having been once fortified from the number of great stones lying all around it, and which they must have used in this way as they are too large for the building of houses."[42]

Matt Field tells an apocryphal little story about the declining days of the village and the legend associated with its hypothetical origins:

"Within forty-five miles of Santa Fé stands a dilapidated town called Pecus [sic], which in its flourishing days must have been inhabited by not less than two thousand souls. The houses now are all unroofed and the walls crumbling. The church alone yet stands nearly entire, and in it now resides a man bent nearly double with age, and his long silken hair, white with the snow of ninety winters, renders him an object of deep interest to the contemplative traveller. The writer with a single American companion once passed a night in this old church, entertained by the old man with a supper of hot porridge made of pounded corn and goat's milk, which we drank with a shell spoon from a bowl of wood, sitting upon the ground at the foot of the ruined altar by the light of a few dimly burning sticks of pine. In this situation we learned from the old man the following imperfect story, which is all the history that is now known of the city of the Sacred Fire.

"The inhabitants of Pecus boasted that they were the chosen people of Montezuma, and in a deep cavern, whose mouth yawns in the hill side behind the church, the sacred fire was kept burning from generation to generation, watched and fed with unwearied vigilance through day And night by the faithful descendants of the great chief. He had said when he left them, 'Montezuma does not die, my children, he goes to wander through happy regions and will again return to bless his people. Take from him this torch of flame, and so long as you suffer not the sacred blaze to expire so long hope to see your chief again, who will then make you a great and happy people and your enemies shall perish; but should this holy fire die, then dies Montezuma and you shall behold him no more!'

"Thus spoke Montezuma before he disappeared, and through hundreds of years the sacred flame continued to blaze in the cavern of Pecus. Man, woman, and child shared the honor of watching the holy fire, and the side of the mountain grew bare as year after year the trees were torn away to feed the consuming torch of Montezuma.

"At length a pestilential disorder came in the summer time and swept away the people. Pecus became a city of mourning, and death with conquering steps strode from dwelling to dwelling. Forms wasting with disease were seen to fall and expire while conveying the dry branches from the mountain side to feed the holy fire. The dying drew forth the dead from the deep cavern, and the last feeble breath of many a victim was given to kindle again the fast expiring flame.

"Gualupeta was the daughter of a grey haired chief, and the betrothed of Josenacio. When the streets of Pecus became silent, and the voice of wailing was no more heard; when the ghastly and unburied forms of the dead outnumbered the beings yet alive; the aged man crept from his bed of pain, and descended from the hollow rock to watch the fire. For the children of Montezuma were passing away, and the sacred flame was almost extinct. Of all Pecus there were now but three to watch the sacred fire, and these were Gualupeta, her father, and lover. Josenacio brought wood from the mountain and sat beside his betrothed feeding the holy fire, while the old man grew weaker hour by hour, until in the deep midnight he expired. Then the heart of the lover failed and he urged Gualupeta to fly from death and abandon the sacred cavern. He was answered by a look which told him that Gualupeta had resolved to die rather than to leave the fire of Montezuma to be extinguished while she had strength to watch it.

"'No, Josenacio,' she said, 'let us die with our people, and be faithful to our sacred trust, and though our race be extinct upon earth, Montezuma will forgive us and we will be happy with him in heaven.'

"Josenacio kissed the faithful girl and sat down by her side to die; and the lovers looked into each other's face to watch the icy fingers of death tracing the pallid colors of the grave. Still midnight was around them and by their side lay the cold form of Gualupeta's father. The red light of the holy fire tinged the cold features of the corpse and with a healthful smile the old man seemed to gaze upon his child. Gualupeta was fast growing faint, and laying her cheek against her lover's, she said.

"'See, Josenacio, my father smiles; he has already seen Montezuma in heaven. Are you not glad that you were faithful?'

"Gualupeta started, for her hand which rested loosely in that of her lover, was clasped with sudden energy. She looked in her lover's face and exclaimed, 'Josenacio, what thought moves you? Why has the lightning kindled in your eye, and why do you press my hand so earnestly?'

"'Gualupeta, the fire of Montezuma shall not yet expire!' exclaimed the youth, and starting to his feet he repeated the words, which were returned distinctly by the hollow echoes of the cavern, sounding like the sacred confirmation of a prophecy.

"'We are dying,' said the maiden, 'how, what can we do to preserve the sacred flame?'

"'We will fire the dry grass of the valley, and the forest that covers the mountain,' exclaimed the youth, 'and over the mighty hills and the far prairies we will spread the destroying flame that shall tell the world how Montezuma's children have passed away.'

"'It is good,' said the maiden.

"'Kiss your father, and let us be gone,' exclaimed lover, and snatching a brand from the fire he caught maiden to his breast and rushed from the cavern.

"A light rose in the sky which was not the light of morning, but the heavens were red with the flames that roared and crackled up the mountain side. And the lovers lay in each other's arms, kissing death from each other's lips, and smiling to see the fire of Montezuma mounting up to heaven.

"That summer passed away, and the winter, and when again the grass was green around the desolate city, two skeletons were found mouldering at the mouth of the cavern. These were Gualupeta and Josenacio, the betrothed lovers, the last watchers at the now extinct fire of Montezuma.

"This is the substance of the old man's story. He told it in glowing words and with a rapt intensity which the writer has endeavored to imitate, but he feels that the attempt is a failure. The scene itself—the ruined church—the feeble old man bending over the ashes, and the strange tones of his thin voice in the dreary midnight—all are necessary to awaken such interest as was felt by the listeners. Such is the story, however, and there is no doubt but that the legend has a strong foundation, in truth; for there stands the ruined town, well known to the *Santa Fé* traders, and there lives the old man, tending his goats on the hill side during the day, and driving them into the church at night. He took from a niche in the wall, small burnt stick and a little clay bowl full of cinders which he said he had himself brought from the bottom of the sacred cavern. That these were actually as he said remnants of the sacred fire there is not the slightest doubt, for from after enquiries we found the history he gave us fully confirmed, and the same story was current among all the Americans residing in *Santa Fé*. It was imperative upon us to leave the place before day light that we might reach our destination (San Miguel) early the next morning, so that we could not gratify our curiosity by descending the cavern ourselves, but we gave the old man a few bits of silver, and telling him that the story with which he had entertained us should be told again in the great United States, we each pocketed a cinder of the sacred fire and departed."[43]

The town had been abandoned recently when Matt visited it. And although it had been plundered a number of times in closing years of occupation, it must have presented an imposing site at the time he viewed it. Today the site is maintained by the Park Service and consists of a few low walls and the thick elevated mass of the cathedral's apse. In the dirt near the pueblo's western edge, my toe uncovered the sole of a moccasin, woven from the fibers of a yucca, and held together only by the support it received in the ground, lying buried for however many centuries it has been since the ancient art gave way to leathercraft.

Pecos Pueblo, 1846 (*Museum of New Mexico*)

Pecos Mission, 1871 (*Museum of New Mexico*)

From a distance riding through the heavy timber on the hillside above the valley floor we could look back through a break and see the church wall, silhouetted by a shaft of light in the cloudy afternoon, a sentinel across the intervening miles and the intervening years, one of the last dramatic reminders against the cascading approach of civilization. Forced out by the density of the pine forest, we picked our way along the rocky slag beside the railroad until we finally abandoned this route for the slight improvement of broken glass and spongy soil beside the highway. An afternoon rain sent us racing into the shelter of a concrete tunnel, the horses hooves thundering upon cement and trumpeting a whining ricochet of echoes. Later when the weather cleared, the afternoon was cool and pleasant and we rode on through the scene of former battles.

Horseman seeking shelter in culvert

That night we camped near the town of Glorieta above Apache Canyon. The worn ruts of the Trail are dimly visible climbing the hill to the west of town. Beside runs the old highway which curves up through the trees to be left hanging above the deep gouge of the Interstate 25. It was our last night's camp and as we relaxed among the alternating meadows and clumps of trees, a sense of nostalgia and transition occupied my mind. The can of beans laced with salty bacon bits seemed especially delicious. The clear sky and the sound of wind in the pines seemed almost fragile as we lay against our saddles and sipped our last grain and orange. And in the morning, after a deep and luxurious sleep, I awoke early to enjoy the spotted light and the sparkle of diamond sunshine on the pine needles. The horses grazing at the end of their long lead ropes drifted slowly through the clearings, looking around, alert and quiet, more reminiscent of game than domesticated servants of man. I pursued them silently, following prints and searching the ground for the hobble which Red had given up in the night until at last I found it and tracked their casual route deeper into the forest. They were headed home to Kansas, and where they reached the fence which we had crossed just prior to camping the night before, I found it on the ground. Their hoof prints led among the trees and past a barn where they had ignored a stack of hay to investigate some ruined curiosities spread around the ground. They looked at me with docility as I approached and followed me without interest as I gathered the ropes and led them back towards camp.

After scouting through the woods and picking up some old glass and nails we mounted and entered Apache Canyon beside the screaming concrete highway. It was hot. The highway and bare rocky hillside sent the heat back and forth through the air until we sweated to match the soapy lather of the horses. Behind me sat Jaffa, her arms wrapped around my stomach in a clammy clasp, reeling occasionally as the debilitating effects of sun crept past her protective clothing. Trotting across especially touchy sections of highway the strap of the canteen broke, tumbled from Jack's pummel and rolled out onto the highway to present a moving obstacle for the dodging speeding cars. At one point shortly after reaching the road two cars went by us at a ferocious speed and one angled over into the lane of the other as though the driver were falling asleep or just not paying attention and in the center lane they slapped sides and began a careening dance between lanes until the initiator recovered his control and the second driver pulled beside the road with a mild case of shock. As Jack rode past the parked car he leaned over and signaled a greeting to the lone driver whose expression conveyed a mixture of daze and anger.

The canyon walls climbed steeply on both sides and were usually barren where they had been cut away to provide an even grade. Below occasionally a sudden stream would cut beneath the highway and open off to the side into a rolling valley with the ancient wagon road and a few adobe buildings. These would have been pleasant interludes in the days of the Trail, but this day they were forgotten in the whizzing directness of our concrete purposes. This road which had always seemed spectacular and serene, one of those highways which can draw a driver out of air-conditioned boredom, began to seem uncomfortable and ugly in the extreme, so different from my early memories of the years before the interstate. Then it had been a drive of tranquility: moonlight framing mesas, cedar and *piñon*, and the towering profile of Starvation Peak; the undulating road reflective of the subtle contours of the land; lone adobes in the night with a soft light penetrating tiny windows, and everywhere a quiet solitude and a sense of place where somehow man just once had seen fit not to conquer. In those times I always had the sense that here one entered a foreign land, somehow un-American in its aboriginal appreciation of unmarred nature.

Ahead were the last bare rocks marking the entrance of Apache Canyon. Here the invading army of 1846 found the abandoned fortifications of Armijo's retreating army. One soldier reported:

> "In about four miles we came to the mouth of (the) pass, a deep canyon with lofty mountains on each side and (with) barely room enough generally for a single wagon, large rocks (being) heaped in confusion all along each side of our way. We passed on through it, a distance of 7 or 8 miles, and at the west end found some timber cut down and a few attempts made at fortification, which the enemy had abandoned the day before. It is a place of great natural strength and could easily be defended by a few men against a whole army, as we have to pass down the canyon with timber and rock all around affording a natural breastwork. Cannon at the mouth can sweep the whole road, as it is almost impossible even for infantry to ascend the precipitous sides of the mountain and attack in the rear, the only way to dislodge troops determined to hold their ground. After passing through and looking back, we were not more astonished that it should be abandoned than glad that the Mexicans who were here yesterday had fled in confusion and disorder and returned to their homes to await events. From information obtained in various ways, it is pretty well ascertained that there were about 3,000 men (not soldiers) at the pass day before yesterday, and that they disagreed amongst themselves, had a fight, and broke up in a row, Armijo with the artillery and some regulars taking the road to the south."[44]

In fact it is said that in negotiations with Armijo five days earlier,

James Magoffin offered him a bribe to disband his troops. Some time later Magoffin submitted a claim to the U.S. Government for "vague" services rendered totaling $50,000.

This spot also saw the most strategic action in the West during the War Between the States, and the pass is more well known for this battle which is called La Glorieta. When William Whitford, the major chronicler of the battle, made his first visits to the area in the late nineteenth century, he encountered a veteran of the Colorado Volunteers who pointed out the various areas along the arroyo and in the trees where he had participated in the heavy fighting back in 1862.

The initial shuffling of loyalties at the beginning of the war saw the great majority of the civilian and military populations of the New Mexico territory remain sympathetic to the Union. Those few officers who switched sides first responded with minor intrigues and efforts to bolster Southern hopes through recruitment of equipment, and then returned South with fancied visions of widespread popular support for the Southern cause in the region. Soon afterwards the Confederate strategists conceived an ingenious plan to occupy the Southwest, link up with Mormon dissidents in Utah, and proceed east through Missouri to join advancing Southern armies in a giant continental pincher movement. The immediate objects of the plan were the forts and munitions of New Mexico, and the mineral wealth of the Colorado and California gold fields.

In December 1861, General H. H. Sibley, C.S.A., left San Antonio, Texas, with 3,500 troops and two batteries of six artillery each. They planned to march up the Rio Grande valley from El Paso del Norte and proceed by Mesilla to occupy the population centers of New Mexico. The hub of the plan was the seizure of the capital of Santa Fe and the supply center at Fort Union on the Santa Fe Trail. The Federal troops under Colonel Canby were assembled at Fort Craig, in south-central New Mexico, and numbered 3,800 including several companies of volunteers and a regiment commanded by Colonel Kit Carson. Sibley decided that an attack on the fort would be too costly and that he would by-pass it in order to draw the troops out for a fight in the open. This Canby sought to avoid fearing that the volunteers would "melt away by desertion" under the pressure of enemy fire. Sibley crossed the river eastward in sight of the fort and camped a mile and a half away. Canby sent 2,500 troops out of the fort to meet the enemy, but panic among the volunteers and refusal of some officers to obey orders led to a disastrous defeat, since known as the battle of Valverde. The Federal troops returned to the fort without surrendering, and the Texans pushed on to Albuquerque to replenish their supplies with aid from sympathetic natives.

There remained a major concentration of supplies at Santa Fe, and in order to keep them from falling into enemy hands, a train of 120 wagons was loaded and sent over the Trail to Fort Union. Soon after the Confederates moved to Santa Fe and set up a permanent headquarters, thus completing a major strategic objective.

Meanwhile, news of Canby's defeat at Valverde was on its way to Governor Gilpin of Colorado where active recruitment of volunteers had already been going on. The First Colorado Volunteers left Denver on February 22nd, the day after the defeat at Valverde, and marching through a foot of snow, reached the Raton mountains two weeks later where they received news of the defeat. Proceeding by forced march they reached Fort Union by the eleventh of March. After spending over a week at the Fort, an advanced unit of 210 cavalry and 180 infantry was sent ahead to surprise the enemy at Santa Fe, spike his guns, and do what damage possible before provoking a major fight. On March 27th these Colorado volunteers, commanded by Major Chivington (on leave from the Methodist ministry), followed the Trail towards Glorieta and at the long rambling adobe structure known as Pigeon's Ranch surprised Confederate pickets who were busy playing cards, taking them prisoner and clearing the way to the canyon. What they didn't realize was that the Texans were already advancing from Santa Fe to seize Fort Union:

> "Descending Apache Canyon for the distance of half a mile, Chivington's force observed the approaching Texans, about six hundred strong, with three pieces of artillery, who, on discovering the Federals, halted, formed line and battery, and opened fire.
>
> "Chivington drew up his cavalry as a reserve under cover, deployed Company D under Captain Downing to the right, and Companies A and E under Captains Wynkoop and Anthony to the left, directing them to ascend the mountain-side until they were above the elevation of the enemy's artillery and thus flank him, at the same time directing Captain Howland, he being the ranking cavalry officer, to closely observe the enemy, and when he retreated, without further orders to charge with the cavalry. This disposition of the troops proved wise and successful. The Texans soon broke battery and retreated down the canyon a mile or more, but from some cause Captain Howland failed to charge as ordered, which enabled the Confederates to take up a new and

strong position, where they formed battery, threw their supports well up the sides of the mountain, and again opened fire.

"Chivington dismounted Captains Howland and Lord with their regulars, leaving their horses in charge of every fourth man, and ordered them to join Captain Downing on the left, taking orders from him. Our skirmishers advanced, and flanking the enemy's supports, drove them pell-mell down the mountainside, when Captain Samuel Cook, with Company F, First Colorado, having been signalled by the major, made as gallant and successful a charge through the canyon, through the ranks of the Confederates and back, as was ever performed. Meanwhile, our infantry advanced rapidly; when the enemy commenced his retreat a second time, they were well ahead of him on the mountainsides and poured galling fire into him, which thoroughly demoralized and broke him up, compelling the entire body to seek shelter among the rocks down the canyon and in some cabins that stood by the wayside."[45]

After collecting and tending to dead and wounded, the Coloradoans fell back to Pigeon's Ranch, dispatching word to Colonel Slough to bring up the main force of 1,312 men for the anticipated battle.

The next day, March 28th, 1862, Slough's main force reached the church at Pecos and formed a joint force of Colorado and New Mexico volunteers as well as regular infantry. At nearby Kozlowski's Ranch they were rejoined by Chivington's command for a final strategic move and engagement. As Slough's main body moved towards the canyon Chivington was ordered to cut around to the western end of Apache Canyon, seize the Galisteo road, and reconnoiter the Confederate position at Johnson's ranch which was located at Cañoncito just beyond the mouth of Apache Canyon.

Arriving there several hours later his troops could hear the cannons indicating the opposing armies had met. Below them 80 wagons were corralled by the stream and guarded by cannon on the hillside commanding the road. With great difficulty they descended the hill and charged the guard. They spiked the gun, ran the train together, blew it up and burned the remains, and bayoneted the mules in the corral. They then returned through the woods having destroyed the Confederates' entire supply of ammunition, equipment and stores.

Meanwhile, the Union forces were a mile west of Pigeon's ranch near the town of Glorieta. The Confederates had thrown a line across the eastern end of the pass opposite them, and the separate artillery began a duel which had been heard by Chivington as well as in Santa Fe 18 miles away. When Union forces tried to sneak up the arroyo on the Confederate left and break past the line, they were repulsed and followed by the whole Confederate line which soon swept beyond the range of its own cannon, forcing the Yankees to retreat and throw up a new line across the Santa Fe Trail in front of Pigeon's Ranch. Heavy attack forced the Union forces onto the ledge behind the house as Yankee grapeshot decimated the Texas line. But the Confederates kept coming, up into the rocks, until the enemy muzzles crossed as they mingled at point blank range among the boulders and trees.

Finally, under cover of darkness, the Union forces began to pull the guns out, one by one, and retreat to the safety of Kozlowski's Ranch seven miles east and just beyond the ruins of Pecos Church. Technically it was a Confederate victory as the Yankees had left the field, but the exertion had been heavy, and they were too exhausted to follow the Yankee retreat. The next day a truce was called as both sides buried their dead up and down the valley, but as the truce time lengthened, the Texans, without food or clothing, decided to fall back to Santa Fe thus halting the strategic advance on Fort Union. They had suffered severe losses and the presence of the unexpected Colorado Volunteers as well as the failure of the population to rally to the cause of the confederacy led to the abandonment of the entire campaign in only a month.

Colonel Slough, not knowing of the Texas retreat, wanted to pursue them but was ordered to fall back to Fort Union, and became so incensed that he soon resigned his command. Five years later, as Chief Justice of the territorial Supreme Court, he was killed in a duel in the billiard room of La Fonda at Santa Fe. Chivington was later promoted and ultimately became a center of controversy for leading the infamous Sand Creek massacre, an ambush of a peaceful Cheyenne Indian village under government protection in eastern Colorado. Under his orders to take no prisoners, his volunteers took every imaginable human part as souvenirs, and when it was over, two thirds of the scalpless dead were women and children. But, by then Chivington, described as "a fine example of a preacher militant," was running for Congress.

William Whitford,[46] who wrote the history of the First Colorado Volunteers, visited and photographed the battlefields along the Santa Fe Trail. Today, 80 years later, much has changed. The railroad runs over the hillside above the chain of meadows where the soldiers battled. The highway passes largely out of sight to the west for a good part of the crossing. The strategic bridge on the Trail, shown in his old photograph, is still there and shows some of the same rock foundations appearing in his photos. But there is no road anymore because the Trail has faded away and the bridge stands decaying and ignored. The meadows have eroded to a point of impassibility by horse or wagon, or have grown up in trees and lost the civilized character which they must have possessed over a century ago when they stood astride the main path between the U.S. and old Mexico.

Pigeon's ranch, Union Headquarters, 1882 (*Museum of New Mexico*)

Pigeon's ranch in 1906 (by Whitford) *(Library State Historical Society of Colorado)*

Trail bridge at Glorieta battlefield in 1906 (by Whitford) *(Library State Historical Society of Colorado)*

The bridge in 1972

Field of the second battle of Glorieta in 1906 (Whitford) *(Library State Historical Society of Colorado*

Battlefield 1972

The Trail entering Apache Canyon from Santa Fe (Whitford, 1906) *(Library State Historical Society of Colorado)*

The entrance in 1972, Chivington came down at right

Johnson's ranch, Confederate headquarters, 1914 *(Museum of New Mexico)*

Site of Johnson's ranch in 1972

Beside the remaining rock walls at what had been Johnson's ranch we stopped to eat. This was the mouth of Apache canyon where Chivington's force had surprised and destroyed the Confederate wagon train. But we made the mistake of asking directions for the Trail which here turned west and followed the stream up the *cañada* (wooded canyon). The irate owner, whose livid commands seemed to reflect some deeper unhappiness than that produced by our unsolicited presence, told us we were trespassing and ordered us back onto the access road away from her property. So now we were away from the Trail and seeking a way through the scrub trees to rejoin it a mile or so west. But each time we stopped to ask a route across, a covetous property owner, isolated in a new plaster-boarded-picture-windowed bungalow would reassure us that the Trail was long since obliterated and to reach the site we would have to traverse private land. Indeed, the Trail was gradually growing up in scrub cedar and *piñon* and only the eroded caliche gravel clearly defined its route. But its obliteration was not primarily physical so much as social: cooperative characteristics which had been required on a difficult and demanding frontier were now giving way to the hostility or indifference of a society in which mindless independence leads to abrasive contact between individuals who all have the same conception how to achieve it.

And so we waited for an uninhabited stretch and crossed the sandy juniper hills until we came to the distinctive ruts. Santa Fe, in the distance, sent a curl of smoke into the sky and we stopped to take a picture of the countryside which almost preserved the past appearance that Gregg experienced arriving 140 years ago. Close to town the road was paved and arrow straight as huge power poles beside dismissed any lingering connection with history. Then, at the last moment, the road curved sharply up into a residential area on the south side of town. That didn't look right. And a brief examination showed the Trail continuing straight across a vacant field beside a monastery, across the road, onto a residential lot where it disappeared into a swimming pool! Following its path down driveways, across the road into the intersection of García and Corrales streets, we could see its deep marks cutting gullies in the otherwise civilized front yards of the city dwellers. We speculated as to whether they knew what had so disturbed the grade in their landscape, but did not stop to ask.

Down the hill beside Camino del Monte Sol, the Trail was angling over towards old College Avenue when we lost it for the last time.

Our landmark and purpose for so many days and minor adventures was now gone as decidedly as those early travelers with whom we had now shared this fascinating journey.

THE END

POSTSCRIPT

It was a century after the railway closed that eastern part of the Trail that we rode it, and now a quarter century has passed since our re-riding. This writing has been a retrospective on my adulthood as well as the changes which have gone on around me. The pundits say that there have been more changes in that 25 years than the previous 100. In reflecting back over the period I've reread a book from that time which coincides with my perspective about some of the changes. I see tremendous population growth in my area which has transformed the cities and countryside; distorting land prices, bringing traffic, congestion, more pressure on the environment, and a general decline in the quality of life. It reminds me of a report I saw which asserted that the carrying capacity of the air, water and resources in the U.S. was 150 million people, a figure we reached in the middle of this century.

Both Jack and I have prospered and we really have no quarrel with the way circumstances have smiled upon us, but I wonder about the opportunities and quality of life for those coming behind. The free swimming holes are fenced in. The spectacular vistas are cabin sites. And the forest has become a commodity to fight over. E. F. Schumacher in his book *Small is Beautiful: Economics as if People Mattered* (1973) describes a culture and value system running out of control. It is a system in which economics dominates, in which profit is the primary goal and efficiency the ultimate measure. Materialism (wealth) comes to define the good life and limitless growth is the ultimate national policy. But in a world in which 5.6% of the population already consumes 40% of the world resources, how can this continue? And certainly it is impossible for the developing world to follow this route out of poverty. Even in the developed world we see cities grow to unmanageable size at the expense of the countryside while its culture and economics colonize the territory around it. The children of the countryside prefer the taste of store-bought bread and eggs to home produced, while Ridlin replaces the nutrition lost and makes children manageable.

Schumacher argues that modern man doesn't experience himself as part of nature, subject to its limitations. We live under the illusion of unlimited power fostered by our scientific and technological achievements. The marketplace becomes our central institution as other considerations subside in the face of this utilitarian calculation of value. Nothing is sacred and everything has its price. Work is stripped of fulfillment and becomes a mechanical, joyless means to an end, motivated only by survival or by envy and greed. The economy is blind to the lack of permanence (sustainability) of this course and society loses its inner cohesion manifesting crime, drug addiction, vandalism, rebellion, homelessness. A few quotes from his book: "The amount of real leisure a society enjoys tends to be in inverse proportion to the amount of labour-saving machinery is employs." "The prestige carried by people in modern industrial society varies in inverse proportion to their closeness to actual production." "Virtually all real production has been turned into an inhuman chore which does not enrich a man but empties him." (This was before our economy forced such a large proportion of women into the labor market to maintain a family's standard of living.)

Ultimately the individual struggles with emptiness as a meaningful inner life is denied and replaced by the guidance of appetite and sensation. Indeed, one author has described our society as "addicted" in our compulsive quest for sublimated satisfactions. To me the most powerful insight into the contemporary psyche has been formulated by John Bradshaw and others under the term "codependency." After the formulations of emotional health developed by Abraham Maslow, I find this concept to be the most useful in understanding myself and others, and it's interesting to me how quick the psychological community has been to dismiss it as an amorphous, imprecise concept.

All this is not to romanticize the often drudging labor of the past or indeed the sometimes precarious nature of survival which accompanied life close to the land. (I have been told the average life span of the Indians was 29 years and for the Mountain Men while living in the Rockies was three.) I know first-hand how remote spiritual and intellectual interests can become when one is faced with exhaustive physical or financial demands. But ultimately our fulfillment is a daily thing and our creativity a result of liberation and flexibility. It has become apparent to me how much we create or deny our opportunities as a result of our personal rigidities or lack of discipline or lack of faith. And it seems to me that foundering values and pressures all around us produce stresses which diminish a real quality of living. It remains to be seen how much the so-called information revolution with its decentralizing forces can counteract the destructive processes around us. There are redeeming potentials.

One simple illustration of a basic value from our heritage: the dignity of the individual. This value calls for respect towards every person and could provide a profound humanizing force in our institutions if it received more than lip service. It would mean no more lies and spies from government; it would profoundly alter salesmanship, manipulative advertising, and the content of television; and it could enhance appropriate appreciation instead of inadvertent abuse towards our children, just to name a few consequences. But could we give up invidious comparison to others, judgments of people we meet, put-downs to enhance our self esteem? And that's just the obstacle at a personal level.

At the societal level it seems to me that we need to organize our society to produce a more "child nurturing" (not "child centered") environment. If it is not safe to be a child, to go out and play without fear of abduction, where neighbors can supplement the attention and models in the family, and where children are not assaulted by images and problems which are beyond their level of maturity, then truly we have created a world at war with itself and the future. This would mean strengthening the bonds of community to counter the singleminded emphasis upon individualism and directing resources to enhance participation in community.

FOOTNOTES

1. Colonel Henry Inman, *The Old Santa Fe Trail* (Topeka: Crane & Co., 1899), pp. 488-490.

2. *Ibid*, p. 53.

3. Augustus Storrs in William E. Brown, *The National Survey of Historic Sites and Buildings;The Santa Fe Trail* (U.S. Dept. of Interior, National Park Service, 1963), p. 141.

4. Inman, *op.cit.*, pp. 13-14.

5. Clyde and Mae Reed Porter, *Matt Field on the Santa Fe Trail*, ed. by John E. Sunder (Norman: University of Oklahoma Press, 1960), pp. 202-203, 213.

6. Susan Sheldon Magoffin, *Down the Santa Fe Trail and into Mexico: the Diary of Susan Shelby Magoffin, 1846-1847*, edited by Stella M. Drumm (New Haven: Yale University Press, 1962), pp. 103-104 (original spelling retained).

7. William H. Emory, *Lieutenant Emory Reports* (Albuquerque: University of New Mexico Press, 1951).

8. Kate L. Gregg, ed., *The Road to Santa Fe: The Journal and Diaries of George Champlin Sibley* (Albuquerque: University of New Mexico Press, 1952).

9. Kenyon Riddle, *Records and Maps of the Old Santa Fe Trail* (Raton, N.M.: *Raton Daily Range*, 1948).

10. Inman, *op.cit.*, pp. 39-40.

11. Josiah Gregg, *Commerce of the Prairies*, edited by Milo Milton Quaife (Lincoln: University of Nebraska Press, 1967), pp. 59-69.

12. Leo E. Oliva, *Soldiers on the Santa Fe Trail* (Norman: University of Oklahoma Press, 1967), pp. 34-36.

13. Otis E. Young, *The First Military Escort on the Santa Fe Trail 1829* (Glendale, Calif.: The Arthur H. Clark Co., 1952), pp. 89-92.

14. *Ibid*, p. 141.

15. Quoted in Inman, *op.cit.*, pp. 76-77.

16. Young, *op.cit.*, p. 144.

17. Josiah Gregg, *op.cit.*, pp. 78-79.

18. Inman, *op.cit.*, pp. 55-59.

19. Kate Gregg, *op.cit.*, p. 88.

20. *Ibid.*, p. 89.

21. Josiah Gregg, *op.cit.*, pp. 70-73.

22. *Ibid.*, pp. 73-75.

23. Kate Gregg, *op.cit.*, pp. 93-94.

24. *Ibid.*, pp. 94-95.

25. Josiah Gregg, *op.cit.*, pp. 77-78.

26. Cited in Inman, *op.cit.*, pp. 69-74.

27. Albert W. Thompson, "Kit Carson's Camp Nichols in the No Man's Land," *Colorado Magazine*, Vol. XI, No. 5 (September 1934), pp. 181-185.

28. Josiah Gregg, *op.cit.*, pp. 13-15.

29. Kate Gregg, *op.cit.*, pp. 97-98 (original spelling retained).

30. Josiah Gregg, *op.cit.*, p. 86.

31. *Ibid.*, pp. 91-97.

32. *Kit Carson's Autobiography*, edited by Milo Milton Quaife (Lincoln: University of Nebraska Press, 1935), pp. 131-135.

33. Inman, *op.cit.*, pp. 166-168.

34. Kate Gregg, *op.cit.*, p. 104.

35. *Ibid.*, pp. 191-192.

36. Porter, *op.cit.*, pp. 265-269.

37. Emory, *op.cit.*, pp. 48-49.

38. Josiah Gregg, *op.cit.*, pp. 225-226.

39. George Rutledge Gibson, *Journal of a Soldier Under Kearny and Doniphan, 1846-47*, edited by Ralph Bieber (Glendale, Calif.: Arthur H. Clark Co., 1935), p. 200.

40. Magoffin, *op.cit.*, p. 98.

41. Field, *op.cit.*, pp. 253-254, 255.

42. Magoffin, *op.cit.*, p. 101.

43. Field, *op.cit.*, pp. 247-251.

44. Gibson, *op.cit.*, pp. 203-204.

45. Inman, *op.cit.*, pp. 196-197.

46. William Whitford, *Colorado Volunteers in the Civil War: The New Mexico Campaign of 1862* (Denver: The State Historical and Natural History Society, 1906, republished in 1963 by Pruett Press, Inc., Boulder, Colorado).